Praise for
How God Makes Men

"Don't we all sometimes feel like there's another man coiled up inside us who desperately wants to get out? In *How God Makes Men*, Pat Morley is going to show you God's way to help you release that man. This isn't just a book. It's a skeleton key to unlock God's master plan for your life. Read it. Apply it. Let God change your life. You're going to love this book!"

— MARK BATTERSON, *New York Times* best-selling author of *The Circle Maker*

"Pat Morley knows men—what they want, what they need, and God's way of helping them get it. Now he has written a watershed book that clearly explains God's role in changing men's lives. After unpacking ten timeless principles of how God forged our Bible heroes, Pat will help you connect the dots to your life today. I highly recommend *How God Makes Men* for your personal reading or small group."

— DR. TONY EVANS, president of the Urban Alternative and senior pastor of Oak Cliff Bible Fellowship

"There are all kinds of help out there to encourage us to be better men. But nothing compares to the manhood wisdom drawn directly from God's Word. And that's what Patrick Morley richly blesses us with in *How God Makes Men*. I highly recommend you drink deeply from it."

— ROBERT LEWIS, founder of Men's Fraternity

"I believe that men are under attack in our culture. Television and other media feed us a steady stream of weak, complacent men—but that's not the kind of man you see in Scripture! All through the Bible, we see stories of bold and brash men who followed God's call into some incredible adventures. In *How God Makes Men,* Patrick Morley reminds us that God still makes those kinds of guys."

—DAVE RAMSEY, *New York Times* best-selling author
and nationally syndicated radio-show host

"This is not a book. It's a gift. Patrick Morley has taken what decades of faithful ministry to men has taught him and laid this wisdom atop the incredibly poignant, true stories of men in the Bible. What God is up to in your life and mine has everything to do with our learning obedience and a faithful walk with Him…while He writes our story. Because of God's grace, our story even has a chance to be epic. Depending on what you and I need right now, this book will be either an encouragement or a necessary kick in the pants."

—DR. ROBERT WOLGEMUTH, best-selling author

"Pat Morley is a masterful teacher of men. *How God Makes Men* is his most ambitious project since his best-selling *Man in the Mirror* twenty-five years ago. It's a fascinating blend of the thousands of up-close-and-personal conversations with men in a variety of circumstances in a turbulent world matched with the stories of ten Bible heroes and how they faced their own strikingly similar issues. There is nothing quite like it!"

—BOB BUFORD, founder of Leadership Network and author
of *Halftime* and *Finishing Well*

"God takes strong men, breaks them down and makes them weak. No man wants to go through this, but this is the path to being used by God. Pat Morley has experienced this and understands the process. For the man who is broken and confused, *How God Makes Men* will bring hope, healing, and biblical clarity. I read it, highlighted it, and marked it up. That to me is the acid test for a valuable book."

—STEVE FARRAR, author of *Point Man*

"No matter how much you already know—or don't know—about God, this captivating book is going to help you grow leaps and bounds in your relationship with Christ. Pat clearly demonstrates how God makes a man by using the personal stories of ten great biblical characters to show us how we, too, can adopt ten life-changing principles that are the trademark of God's man. Pat's knowledge and passion to help every man be the person God created him to be makes *How God Makes Men* a must-read!"

—KYLE VANN, energy consultant and retired CEO
   of Entergy-Koch LP

for them to become" is for you too. And it's one of the main features we'll be exploring together.

How did God mold and mobilize these men? What were the obstacles they faced? What held them back? How did God get them uncoiled? And what was their part? As we spend time listening to their lives, we will come face to face with the gritty truth that can release and sustain the passion of our faith too. When added together, they're not just ten amazing stories but one big story—yours!

Here's the promise of *How God Makes Men*. And it's a huge one. If you will absorb and embrace the timeless principles offered by these ten men, you can get past the shallow cultural Christianity that wants to gut your manhood and get to—or back to—a more biblical Christianity.

If you will let these ten men mentor you, then, like them, *you* will become the man God created you to be. *You* will release the power of God in every direction and detail of your life. *You* will know how to sustain the passion of your faith. And *you* will be well on the way to writing your own epic story. Why? Because God is way too good to let our lives merely turn out like we planned!

You always knew that one day you would be called upon to take your place on the battlefront, right? This is that call. Together, we can turn this around. This is a battle we can win. We cannot, we must not, and by God's grace we will not fail.

If this is what you want, turn the page. I have some guys I want you to meet.

ABRAHAM

THE PRINCIPLE OF BELIEVING GOD ANYWAY

HOW GOD MAKES A MAN'S FAITH STRONGER

James and Brandy both went into their marriage fully intending to build their life together on the rock of Christ. James, who attends the Bible study I teach, told me, "And so it went… at first."

After five carefree years without kids, they started a family with two wonderful children, anticipating that life would only get happier. But in reality the demands of work and the stress of raising children began to take a toll on their marriage. They lost that important feeling of being close to your soul mate. That made it easier to dwell on each other's faults, and so they slowly drifted apart. At the fourteen-year mark, weakened by self-pity over his unhappiness at home, James fell into the arms of another woman. When confronted by friends over his adultery, he said, "I felt like I was being torn in two."

With the help of their church community, James and Brandy reconciled and started over. But this transgression, along with the unresolved issues each had brought into their marriage, kept eating away at them. For his part, James was quick to anger and wore his feelings on his sleeve. Brandy, in contrast, buried her feelings because she thought that was the Christian thing to do.

When the children hit their teens, James and Brandy decided to get counseling to help them become better parents. But those conversations opened a can of worms. His affair came back to center stage. Their arguments became more and more frequent. Brandy, particularly, seemed annoyed at every little thing James did.

One day James said to her, "Brandy, if these things bother you so much, then why don't you ask me to leave?" So she did.

After a few days of living alone, James realized what a horrible mistake he had made. His repeated pleas for reconciliation fell on deaf ears. Brandy was boiling with a volcanic anger, and she wanted nothing to do with him. In the months that followed, he found e-mails that revealed his wife was getting emotionally attached to an old flame. That attachment eventually led to an affair.

James still believed God wanted them to reconcile and stay married. But after everything that had gone on, he was thinking, *You've got to be kidding me. How could that possibly happen now?* Brandy clearly despised him, and she had opened her heart to the other man. There appeared to be no way his marriage could recover.

He started losing weight and couldn't sleep. He routinely woke up at around 3:00 a.m. and pleaded with God to save his marriage.

One morning God whispered to his heart, "James, I have you. But you need to give Brandy to Me."

James wasn't sure what that meant. He said, "How can I give her up when what I really need to do is win her back?"

Meanwhile, Brandy continued moving away from James. She began bringing up the topic of divorce in their infrequent communications, though James resisted it every time. He wanted to find some way to get Brandy back, but he didn't know how to begin.

One day James yelled at the top of his lungs, "God, I don't think I can hold out any longer!"

When he was done venting, he heard God whisper, "Are you finished?"

Then, "Wait."

One day, after a couple of years of separation, Brandy sent James a text: "Happy Father's Day." For an hour James sobbed uncontrollably and cried out to God to bring his marriage back from the dead. Later that day, when James picked up his daughter for dinner, Brandy asked if she could join them. They had a wonderful evening talking and laughing.

The two started dating again. Each saw changes in the other. Then they went to counseling together and began learning how to open up and express honest feelings without letting their emotions become destructive. They sought and received forgiveness from each other.

After two years of prayer and pain and waiting on God, James and Brandy got back together.

And here's what I don't want you to miss: in his darkest times, James did not see how God could possibly bring to pass what he hoped for—the restoration of his marriage. But he did his best to keep trusting God during the wait. And in His time, God did what seemed impossible.

But God didn't bring about this dramatic turnaround overnight. It was a process—a process that took time. "Bible Time," actually, as you'll soon see. God's goal in this process was to release unwavering faith in Him.

To that end, He is going to take each of us through a similar process of transformation, though your personal issues will most likely be very different from what James went through. God graciously "forces" our faith to grow by creating or permitting situations that require us to find reserves of faith we don't even know we have. And through that process, we become stronger, wiser men. We become men of faith. Men who are increasingly conformed to the image of Christ. How does it happen? By the process described in the first of the ten principles we'll be looking at together in *How God Makes Men:*

> God makes men by showing us how we can believe Him anyway in the face of what seem like impossible circumstances.

What is God calling you to trust Him for that makes you say, "Are You kidding me, God? How could that possibly happen?"

Whatever it is, you're not alone. There is no Christian alive who always has faith and never doubts. Run from anyone who tells you differently. It's normal to have doubts. But by the end of this chapter, you will see how God wants to forge us into men who can believe Him anyway, even when we've really messed up. Even when our circumstances seem impossible.

So let's get to it.

If you think James messed up—if you think *you've* messed up—consider this guy.

A FLAWED MAN
AMONG FLAWED MEN

While writing this chapter, I spent many hours with a man who once encouraged his wife to sleep with another man so he could get ahead. He also fathered a child with his housekeeper and later cut them both off financially. Once, when he was surrounded by thugs who had their eyes on his pretty wife, he pretended to be single to avoid getting roughed up.

What kind of man would do those things?

Would you be surprised to learn I'm talking about Abraham, the father of our faith (see Romans 4:16)?

As I implied in the preface, none of the ten men we'll be looking at in this book were perfect. Not even close. These men were flawed—like us. They learned and grew over time—like us. That's what makes their stories so perfect for us to study. Bit by bit, God made them more nearly into the men He wanted them to be—just like He does with us. Let's face it. If God didn't work with flawed men, He wouldn't have any to work with at all.

So why, precisely, did the Holy Spirit include the story of Abraham in the Bible? I can tell you one reason why. Abraham faced three different tests that, by degrees, you and I will also face—if we haven't already.

Let's take them one at a time.

Going Not Knowing

Abraham spent most of his life in the city of Ur, located in what is now southern Iraq. A major population center, Ur boasted a robust economy and vibrant culture.

At seventy-five years old, Abraham was healthy, wealthy, and active, with lots of friends, relatives, and employees to share his life with. But he and his wife, Sarah, were childless—a deep pain for both of them.

Abraham no doubt looked forward to his golden years. With the climate of Scottsdale, Ur might have made the list of "Ten Best Places to Retire." Except for having no heir, everything else felt familiar and comfortable. But Abraham's plans were about to change dramatically.

One day God delivered a message to him that would upend the rest of his life. The Lord said, "Leave your country, your people and your father's household and go to the land I will show you" (Genesis 12:1).

Try to imagine Abraham's shock at hearing the voice of his Creator. First, God told him to leave everything that was familiar. Second, He didn't tell Abraham where he was going. "I'm not going to tell you where you're going just yet. I'll let you know." But if Abraham answered the call, God promised:

> I will make you into a great nation
>> and I will bless you;
> I will make your name great,
>> and you will be a blessing.

I will bless those who bless you,

 and whoever curses you I will curse;

and all peoples on earth

 will be blessed through you. (verses 2–3)

This was the first test God put to Abraham: Will you believe God's great promise for an invisible future or cling to the visible present?

We know what Abraham did. "Abram left, as the LORD had told him" (verse 4). The book of Hebrews puts it succinctly: "By faith Abraham, when called to go to a place he would later receive as his inheritance, obeyed and went, even though he did not know where he was going" (Hebrews 11:8).

By faith.

Obeyed and went.

Even though he did not know where he was going.

This is not some crazy, ancient idea. It's part of the normal Christian life. God routinely tests our faith as part of the process by which He makes men. The question this test puts to us is this: Will we believe His promise or cling to what we know? Will we leave what's familiar—if that's what He calls us to do—for the promise of a better future?

Faith is letting the reality of the unseen rule over the unreality of the seen. To leave the familiar present for an unknown future is a supreme test of faith—but it is the kind of faith God rewards. That's what Bill and Sherry did when they gave up their personal comfort to adopt an Asian orphan. That's what Fernando did when he went back to school to learn a new trade that would provide for his family after his factory job went away. That's what Jake and his family did when they left their familiar church to be part of a new church plant. How about you? Is God asking you to trust Him with something? Will you believe God's great promise for an invisible future or cling to the visible present?

Abraham passed his first test, and I hope you will pass yours too when it's your turn. But God was far from finished making Abraham into the man He had created him to be. An even bigger test was right around the corner. And again, it's a test that applies to us too.

THE TWENTY-FIVE-YEAR WAIT

God's plan for our lives is revealed in stages, as Abraham discovered. God sent him to the land of Canaan, but then a famine forced him to move to Egypt. Later, when he returned, he established a large free-range herding operation. Once again, he was enjoying a comfortable existence—one of the leading men of the area.

Still, something was spoiling the satisfaction of the life he was living. And frankly it seemed to fly in the face of the promise God had given him—the promise that God would make him into a great nation. How could that be, when he and Sarah were childless?

So one night God took Abraham outside and told him to look up at the heavens and count the stars. I'm sure it was a clear night, like a special night our family experienced on the Blue Ridge Parkway. We stopped our car, shut off the motor, got out, and looked up into a sky bulging with stars that dangled so close we felt as though we could reach out and pick one, like an apple or an orange. The majesty of the heavens overwhelmed us. I imagine that's how Abraham felt that night as he looked up.

As Abraham was drinking in the spectacle of an uncountable number of stars, God said to him, "So shall your offspring be" (Genesis 15:5).

God tested the faith of Abraham again. His second test was this: Will you trust God to do what seems impossible? After all, how could he father offspring? He was well over seventy-five years old, and his wife was barren. They had been trying to have a child for many, many years. What reason was there to believe they would have a child now?

Abraham had to decide. To believe this crazy promise God gave him about the stars and his offspring. Or not.

Again, we know what Abraham did. Verse 6 says, "Abram believed the LORD, and he credited it to him as righteousness." That single moment is why the New Testament repeatedly calls Abraham the father of our faith. He believed God in the face of unbelievable circumstances.

But the test wasn't over. A decade after the promise made to him that star-studded night, Abraham *still* didn't have a son!

That's when Abraham once again revealed his flawed humanity. His wife coaxed him into sleeping with their housekeeper, Hagar, who got pregnant and had a son, Ishmael. For years Hagar taunted Sarah because she had a child and Sarah didn't. When Sarah couldn't take it anymore, she demanded that her husband banish Ishmael and Hagar. And he did. He put them out.

Now fast-forward to Abraham at ninety-nine years of age. It was now twenty-four years since he had left his homeland, and yet he still had no heir. But again God reaffirmed the promise that he would have a son with Sarah (see Genesis 17:1–16).[1]

Abraham's first reaction? He laughed. The Bible tells us exactly what he was thinking: "Will a son be born to a man a hundred years old? Will Sarah bear a child at the age of ninety?" (verse 17).

Put that way, it does seem laughable. But even though twenty-four years had passed since the promise was made, Abraham continued to believe in the face of unbelievable circumstances. He passed the second test and was rewarded with a son, Isaac, just as God had promised.

As Hebrews 11:11 tells us, "By faith Abraham, even though he was past age—and Sarah herself was barren—was enabled to become a father because he considered him faithful who had made the promise."

A long test is obviously more difficult to pass than a short test. It's one thing to have faith in God if He delivers on His promise quickly. But as the years roll by, it's human nature to assume, *I guess I heard wrong.*

I'll give you an example. Chris, a thirty-two-year-old single man who loves to work with children, said to me, "I know my purpose. It's to be a husband and father. But I feel like something is blocking me." He became a committed Christian in college. Then five years ago God called him to move to Orlando. He said, "I thought it was to find a wife, start a family, and settle down. But now I'm not so sure."

Most men I know can point to something they believed God was calling them to—something He promised, something they believed they were led to pursue. For some, it's to get married and have or adopt children. For others, it's to go to college or start their own businesses or change careers. Still others sense God calling them to move to another city or go into ministry.

But now it's five, ten, fifteen, or more years later and they're still waiting. They've begun to doubt. They think, *Maybe I didn't hear from God after all. Maybe I just imagined it. Or maybe I've let God down and*

He's changed His mind about giving me this thing. There's a blockage somewhere. It's just not happening. Or so it seems. What's going on?

Here's the advice I give them: start thinking in Bible Time.

THINKING IN BIBLE TIME

God has an altogether different way of looking at time than we do. As Peter said, "With the Lord a day is like a thousand years, and a thousand years are like a day" (2 Peter 3:8). In "earth time" Jesus died two thousand years ago. But in Bible Time it was only the day before yesterday.

Bible Time is elastic. At our Bible study I asked a couple of men to measure the length of a bungee cord. It was two feet. Then I asked them to stretch it as far as they could and remeasure. This time it was five feet. So which was it: two feet or five feet? It was both. What may seem like an eternity to us can be like the blink of an eye to God.

Though Abraham no doubt felt as if twenty-five years was a long time, it wasn't much in Bible Time. From the time God promised a new country to Abraham, it took nearly 500 earth years for that promise to be fulfilled—430 years of slavery in Egypt and 40 years of wandering through the wilderness. But in Bible Time, God fulfilled His promise by noon!

Suppose you and I meet for breakfast at 7:30 a.m. I ask you, "What do you want more than anything else in the world that is righteous, pure, noble, and honors God?" Let's say you share your dream and calling to become a godly man, husband, and father.

Now imagine I hold the power to make that happen. Suppose I say, "I love and care about you so much that I promise to make your dream come true." If I could give you the thing you want most in life, would you be willing to wait until noon? How about for an hour? How about for ten minutes? In Bible Time, ten minutes could be ten years.

Thinking in Bible Time will give you an eternal perspective and help you manage expectations. Also, when you think in Bible Time, verses like this one make more sense: "We do not lose heart. Though outwardly we are wasting away, yet inwardly we are being renewed day by day. For *our light and momentary troubles* are achieving for us an eternal glory that far outweighs them all" (2 Corinthians 4:16–17).

Bible Time has many practical applications. I meet men all the time who are so impatient for change that they are making huge decisions— to close a business, to cut off a child, to divorce a wife, to bail out on a home mortgage—because they are impatient. They are not willing to wait on God. They don't have a concept of Bible Time.

How about you? Whatever God has called you to start, pull an Abraham. Reset your clock and don't give up. God is testing you. He might test you for decades. Will you trust God to do what seems impossible? Whatever is not happening that you believed God was going to do, here's my advice: Give it a few more years. Give God a chance to bring glory to Himself by fulfilling your longing.

Once you embrace Bible Time as the norm, it takes off a lot of pressure. It's the kingdom perspective on time that will not only help keep your faith intact but help release the power of God in every direction and detail of your life. Cru founder Bill Bright loved to say, "Faith is like a muscle. The more you exercise it, the bigger it grows." That's a good thing, because Abraham would need it. God would soon put him to the ultimate test of faith.

MAKING THE ULTIMATE SACRIFICE

Abraham was now well over one hundred years of age. (There are no expiration dates on growing in faith.) He was living in Beersheba, an area at the northern edge of the Negev desert where his herds could roam freely. Again God came and spoke to him. This time His command was truly shocking: "Take your son, your only son, Isaac, whom you love, and go to the region of Moriah. Sacrifice him there as a burnt offering on one of the mountains I will tell you about" (Genesis 22:2).

This may not have sounded quite as insane to Abraham as it does to us, because many pagan religions of his time sacrificed children. But it was terrible nevertheless. As God Himself made very clear, He was asking him to sacrifice not just any child but his own son—the one he had waited to hold in his arms for a quarter century. The only one he would ever have with Sarah. The one he loved more than his own life.

Abraham must have thought, *God, I don't understand. I believed You. My wife wept herself to sleep night after night because we couldn't have children. I carried that ache around for decades. I trusted You for the thing I wanted so much—this son—and by a miracle You gave him to me. Now You are asking me to do what?*

The third test God put to Abraham could be expressed this way: Are you willing to give God the one thing you most want to keep?

Whatever else was going through his mind, he obeyed immediately. Without delaying, "early the next morning" Abraham got up, took Isaac and a couple of servants with him, and headed to Moriah (verse 3). Before long, he came to the hill identified by God for the sacrifice. His servants waited at a distance, out of sight of the bizarre scene about to be enacted on the hilltop. He tied up his son Isaac with ropes and put him on a pile of firewood that he had arranged on the large rock that would double as an altar.

Abraham had a knife in his hands. He may have hesitated, but he wasn't going to disobey. His testing over the years had built his faith muscle until it was like the bicep of a bodybuilder. As Abraham took the knife in his hand, and at the last possible moment, the angel of the Lord cried out to him from heaven: "Abraham! Abraham!" The angel went on, "'Do not lay a hand on the boy,' he said. 'Do not do anything to him. Now I know that you fear God, because you have not withheld from me your son, your only son'" (verses 11–12).

Again Hebrews summarizes the story for us:

By faith Abraham, when God tested him, offered Isaac as a sacrifice. He who had received the promises was about to sacrifice his one and only son, even though God had said to him, "It is through Isaac that your offspring will be reckoned." Abraham reasoned that God could raise the dead, and figuratively speaking, he did receive Isaac back from death. (Hebrews 11:17–19)

Abraham got his son back. You see, the test was never that God was going to take away his son. The test was always about whether Abraham was *willing to let Him.*

One thing we can say for sure. No matter how severely God may test your faith, you will never be tested more than He tested Abraham. But His reasons are the same. The test God put to Abraham is the same one Jesus puts to us: Are you willing to give up the one thing you most want to keep?

For many of us, the one thing we most want to keep is our own lives, especially if we're comfortable. But the gospel of Jesus calls on us to give up our lives and follow Him with our whole hearts, which is exactly what Abraham did. So where did Abraham get his radical faith? There's only one way that will ever happen. That kind of absolute loyalty can come only from putting our complete faith in Jesus Christ. Jesus said, "Your father Abraham rejoiced at the thought of seeing my day; he saw it and was glad" (John 8:56). Some call this radical, and of course it is, but it's also the way the Bible describes the normal Christian life. And there is no "second" way. There is only "the" way. We'll have a lot more to say about this as we go along, but that's exactly the kind of radical faith in God that Abraham had and that, by following his example, we can have too.

What are you hanging on to that keeps you from fully trusting Christ with the details of your life? Like James at the beginning of the chapter, what is your "Brandy" that you need to give back to God? That is the thing He is asking you to let go of.

GROWING YOUR FAITH MUSCLE

My first calling was as a real estate developer, and I loved it. It made me feel alive. But then the Orlando office market became seriously overbuilt. Vacancies hit an all-time record. A major tenant moved out of one of our office buildings. As hard as we tried, we just could not find a replacement.

One of my investors had too much of his money in that one deal, and he came unglued. He started spreading rumors and threatened a lawsuit. It got to me. At that point I didn't have much faith in myself and I barely knew God. The situation seemed impossible, humanly speaking. I thought for sure this investor was going to splash my name all over town, my reputation would be ruined, and that would be the end of my real estate career. Before long, I also started to question my faith in God.

Then one day I read,

> Have no fear of sudden disaster
>   or of the ruin that overtakes the wicked,
> for the Lord will be your confidence
>   and will keep your foot from being snared.
>   (Proverbs 3:25–26)

My chest started to pound. The Lord spoke to my heart, and I believed God in the face of unbelievable circumstances—only a little at first. It was just a baby step, but I took it.

My little bit of faith must have been at least as big as a mustard seed because I found the courage to carry on. Even though the business deal got worse, not better, I was able to resolve my problems with the investor without legal action. And my faith grew.

So the next time you're in a situation where God asks you to strike out into unknown territory, or He makes you wait far longer than seems normal, or He asks you to give up so much that you wonder if it's worth the cost, pull an Abraham. Believe God anyway in the face of what seem like impossible circumstances.

That's one of the main ways He is making you into the man He wants you to be. The more you use your faith muscle, the bigger it will get.

The advantage of walking with God in faith over the years is that you actually come to a place where it is harder to doubt than believe, because you have seen Him act so many times before. That's what has happened to me over the many years that have passed since that miracle in my early real estate days. That's what happened to Abraham. And maybe that has already happened to you. If not, God most definitely wants that to be your experience too.

So, what has God called you to do that may look outrageous? You may have no idea what you're getting into.

The question He is asking you is simple: Will you do it anyway?

For Reflection and Discussion

1. What is God calling you to trust Him for that makes you say, "Are You kidding me, God? How could that possibly happen?"

2. What was the operative principle in Abraham's life according to Hebrews 11:8, 11, and 17? How did that principle play out in the three tests we looked at in this chapter?

3. Which of Abraham's three tests—or some other test—are you currently facing? How is God showing you that you can believe Him anyway in the face of what seem like impossible circumstances?

2

JOSEPH

THE PRINCIPLE OF
A GREATER GOOD

How God Shapes Men
for a Higher Purpose

Steve's career has been a wild ride. After becoming the youngest store manager in the history of a national chain, he was forced out because of an internal power struggle. That was a decade ago. Since then he has bounced from one job to another, none of which has even remotely measured up to his store manager position.

Steve put on a brave face and pretended he was okay with it for several years. *After all,* he thought, *I'm a Christian, and Christians are supposed to trust God and persevere.* But finally he just couldn't hold it in any longer. His confidence was shattered, and he felt like a failure. He told his wife, "I've never felt farther from God. I feel like He has abandoned me."

We can all relate, can't we? I know I can. I felt it every single day for seven grueling years when I fought for survival in business. You may be in a difficult marriage, feel you're stuck in a job that's going nowhere, have not spoken to family members for so long you're embarrassed about it, suffer with a handicap or long-term illness, or have been upside down financially for so long you've lost hope. You pray and pray, but nothing changes. In fact, things often get worse, not better. You can't get your life to add up.

At times like that, who hasn't thought, *What's going on here?* We think, *If God loves me, He's got a funny way of showing it.*

Nothing is more painful than feeling you've been abandoned by God.

Let me ask you a question. Please be as honest with yourself as you can in answering it. Do you really believe that God is faithfully at work in your life today—leading you, shaping you, and remaking you into a more complete man for His glory? It's hard to believe, isn't it, when your circumstances seem out of control?

God has good news for you. It's the second principle of *How God Makes Men:*

> God makes men by orchestrating
> even the toughest circumstances
> of our lives for a greater good.

The biblical story of Joseph beautifully illustrates how this principle works. In this chapter you'll learn the remarkable truth that empowered Joseph to get on top of his feelings of abandonment and to finish strong. Joseph's life didn't add up either, until the day he finally understood how the often-difficult events of his life fit into God's larger redemptive plan. I believe you'll find it to be a hopeful and liberating message for your own life.

CAUGHT IN THE UPS AND DOWNS

Like Steve in his highly successful job, Joseph appeared to be on a fast track to success. That is, until the day his ten brothers surprised him by selling him into slavery.

I'm not making this up.

Here's how it started. Joseph's father loved him more than his brothers, and they were incensed with jealousy. Their jealousy turned to hatred when Joseph told them about two dreams he'd had that seemed to predict he would rule over his family.

When the brothers saw an opportunity to get rid of him, they sold seventeen-year-old Joseph to a caravan headed for Egypt, where he was purchased by Potiphar, the captain of Pharaoh's guard. Joseph was ripped from his father, caged like an animal, and sold into slavery. It's the first mention in the Bible of human trafficking. If we saw a human-interest story about the pain and suffering of this seventeen-year-old boy on the evening news, I'm sure we'd all get a little misty.

But in all that gut-wrenching sorrow, the story took a surprising turn. The Bible says,

> *The LORD was with Joseph and he prospered,* and he lived in
> the house of his Egyptian master. When his master saw that
> the LORD was with him and that *the LORD gave him success in*

everything he did, Joseph found favor in his eyes and became his attendant. Potiphar put him in charge of his household, and he entrusted to his care everything he owned. (Genesis 39:2–4)

What's going on here? If "the LORD was with [Joseph]" and "gave him success in everything he did," why had God allowed his brothers to do such a wicked thing to him? But things are rarely what they seem to be, as we'll soon discover.

Joseph's troubles were far from over. Potiphar's wife was powerful, wealthy, and probably beautiful. I think she was used to getting what she wanted—and what she wanted next was young, handsome Joseph. So she set about to seduce him.

Every time he turned around, there she was, coming on to him, luring him with another proposition. It's not hard to imagine how much pressure Joseph was under. Although Potiphar's wife had nothing to lose, Joseph had everything to lose—his integrity, his work, maybe his life. Joseph knew he owed loyalty to this woman's husband.

But right choices don't always end up with happy outcomes. When she couldn't have her way, Potiphar's wife made him pay, accusing Joseph of trying to rape her. Potiphar was furious and threw him into prison.

Yet once again God took an evil and turned it around. Genesis 39:20–21 says, "But while Joseph was there in the prison, *the LORD was with him; he showed him kindness and granted him favor* in the eyes of the prison warden."

Before long the warden put Joseph in charge of everything, just as Potiphar had done. So even though Joseph was in prison, God looked after him. But still we may wonder: If the favor of God was with Joseph, why was he sold into slavery, falsely accused of rape, and thrown into jail in the first place?

Again, things are rarely as they appear to be. Something bigger—something with eternal consequences—was going on here.

THE DAY THAT CHANGED EVERYTHING

While Joseph was serving the warden, two of Pharaoh's officials—a cupbearer and the chief baker—were jailed. They had mysterious dreams, and Joseph interpreted them. His predictions came true—the chief baker was killed and the cupbearer was restored to his work in the palace.

Time passed, Joseph still behind bars for a crime he didn't commit. But when Pharaoh had two terrible dreams that no one could interpret, the cupbearer remembered Joseph and told Pharaoh about him. Pharaoh ordered that Joseph be brought from jail to interpret his dream too.

Standing there before Pharaoh, the slave-turned-prisoner made an astonishing prediction from the ruler's dreams. "You will have seven years of unbelievable prosperity," he said, "and then there will be seven years of famine throughout the whole area. It will be terrible. What I recommend is that you find the wisest man you can and appoint him to organize Egypt so that you will be ready for the famine" (see Genesis 41:29–33).

On that day, Joseph's story suddenly took another dramatic turn that changed everything. Pharaoh asked, "Who better to do this than Joseph? He is the wisest man I know" (verses 38–40). That's how, at the age of thirty, Joseph became the second most powerful man in Egypt.

Follow what happens next in Joseph's story, and you'll get a clear picture of what God had in mind from the beginning.

The prosperity began, just as Joseph had predicted, and during the next seven years he collected so much grain that he stopped keeping records. Then, also as he had predicted, famine struck. Two years went by and the famine spread throughout the region as far away as Canaan, where Joseph's family lived. Joseph's father told his sons, "Go down to Egypt to buy some grain so we don't die" (see 42:2).

They did go down and made an appointment with Joseph to buy grain. When they walked in, he recognized his brothers immediately, but they didn't recognize him. Joseph put them through a series of rigorous tests, but he didn't reveal who he was until his brothers brought his younger brother, Benjamin, back down to Egypt. Genesis 45:1–3 tells us,

> Joseph could no longer control himself before all his attendants, and he cried out, "Have everyone leave my presence!" So there was no one with Joseph when he made himself known to his brothers. And he wept so loudly that the Egyptians heard him, and Pharaoh's household heard about it.
>
> Joseph said to his brothers, "I am Joseph! Is my father still living?"

You can taste the anguish, can't you? These were the same brothers who had wickedly sold him like a dog when he was seventeen.

"They bruised his feet with shackles, his neck was put in irons" (Psalm 105:18). At this point Joseph was thirty-nine years old. So twenty-two long years had passed. He never expected to see his family again. And yet here his brothers were.

If you've ever felt abandoned by others and by God, you can empathize with Joseph, can't you? Maybe you've gone through trouble after trouble, suffering after suffering. You have prayed and prayed, yet nothing has changed. Yes, you have God in your life. Yes, He has given you favor here and there. But a cloud of uncertainty still looms over you. What do you do with that?

Joseph's story is for you. Let me show you what I mean.

When Purpose Becomes Visible

What happened next struck Joseph like lightning. God revealed a truth—an insight—so astonishing and so liberating that it gave purpose and meaning to every moment of the entire twenty-two years he had spent in exile and suffering. Here it is: *Nothing that happens to us by human decision can ever happen apart from the will of God.* Does that sound overstated? Let me show you how it's completely true—so true that you can stake your life on it. Listen to Joseph put this powerful principle in his own words:

> I am your brother Joseph, the one you sold into Egypt! And now, do not be distressed and do not be angry with yourselves for selling me here, *because it was to save lives that God sent me ahead of you.* For two years now there has been famine in the

land, and for the next five years there will not be plowing and reaping. *But God sent me ahead of you to preserve for you a remnant on earth and to save your lives by a great deliverance.*

So then, it was not you who sent me here, but God. (Genesis 45:4–8)

Until that very moment, Joseph didn't know he was part of God's larger redemptive plan. But the Lord suddenly opened his eyes, and finally his purpose became visible. He saw the much higher purpose for the tragedy God had allowed. Three times he repeated it!

God revealed to Joseph that He had been sovereignly orchestrating all of the seemingly random circumstances of his life for a greater good. And when that happened, it gave meaning and purpose to all those years when he felt as though God was so far away.

And that goes for us too. That's why this story is in the Bible. God wants us to know that He is in control. He doesn't do "random." He is not caught off guard by our sufferings. Yes, He allows things we do not understand. But He is permitting things for a greater good that someday, in His grace and loving-kindness, He will enable us to understand, just like He did for Joseph.

That's what happened to me.

I quit high school in the middle of my senior year and joined the army. I couldn't wait to get away. My brothers and I fought constantly, and being the oldest, I always seemed to get the switch. I hated them for it.

Many anguish-filled years later, after I became a Christian, I was able to lead my brother Robert to Christ before he died of a heroin overdose. I also had the privilege of leading both of my parents to Christ (or back to Christ, I'm not sure) before they died. And my brother Pete has become a dedicated Christian. God used me as part of His larger redemptive plan to graft the gospel into my family line for generations to come.

A big part of my purpose became visible. God had me in mind. But more than that, He had my whole family in mind.

In due time God's purpose in your life will become visible too, if it hasn't already.

You Are Under His Protection

Until He makes your purpose visible, however, your comfort is to know that nothing can ever happen to you apart from the will of God. He knows everything about you. Matthew 10:29 says, "Are not two sparrows sold for a penny? Yet not one of them will fall to the ground apart from the will of your Father."

From cover to cover, the Bible teaches that nothing happens apart from the will of God. Nothing. That doesn't mean God is necessarily *causing* the thing that's happening to you. He may be, but it's just as likely that someone is using his or her free will to do something evil to you and God is allowing that to happen for a greater good.

In theology this is called *the doctrine of meticulous providence,* or "the greater good" doctrine. It states that God will allow no evil except that which prevents a greater evil or brings about a greater good.

This is the beautiful truth Joseph understood that triggered his emotional explosion. Whatever happens to us is always within the circle of God's will, purpose, and plan. And whatever happens, we can know that God will use it for good. We are all familiar with Romans 8:28: "In all things God works for the good of those who love him, who have been called according to his purpose."

God will categorically never allow any evil to touch His disciples unless it is something that He is going to work for good. Even if it takes a very long time. If He won't let a sparrow fall to the ground apart from His will, how much more will He watch over us? You see, while God is making us into the men He created us to be, we are each under the protection of His meticulous providence.

SHOWERS IN THE DESERT

I've noticed in my own life that even during the long, hard years, God was always there. I see the same thing in Joseph's story. And I believe it will be true for you as well.

The Lord will encourage you in big and little ways—a kind word at work that cheers you up, a special time in prayer or reading your Bible, a friend who asks you to lunch with no agenda, warm times with your family. In those special moments you will sense His goodness or will be reminded that He hasn't forgotten you. These times may feel too brief. But they're real—like a cloud bursting open in the desert that makes flowers bloom in the least likely places.

Think of it like this: When God sends you on a mission, He will also send His favor. Look at the strong connection between God's favor to Joseph and the mystery-shrouded mission God sent him on:

- "The LORD was with Joseph and he prospered" (Genesis 39:2).
- "The LORD gave him success in everything he did, Joseph found favor" (39:3–4).

- "The LORD was with him; he showed him kindness and granted him favor" (39:21).
- "The warden paid no attention to anything under Joseph's care, because the LORD was with Joseph and gave him success in whatever he did" (39:23).
- "It was to save lives that God sent me ahead of you" (45:5).
- "God sent me ahead of you" (45:7).
- "It was not you who sent me here, but God" (45:8).

The simple truth is that we can endure almost any amount of pain if we believe it has a purpose.

Chuck Colson told a story in *Kingdoms in Conflict* about some prisoners in a Nazi concentration camp.[1] Every day they were forced to fill wheelbarrows with sand and push them from one end of the prison yard to the other, then empty them. The next day they put the sand back in the wheelbarrows, pushed them back to where they started the day before, and emptied them again. This went on day after day.

The prisoners started going crazy. One man collapsed and began to sob uncontrollably. Another man ran into the electric fence and was electrocuted. Why? Because there was no purpose in their ordeal. It was a form of torture.

You may be enduring something right now that makes no sense to you. It feels like torture. But God has given us the story of Joseph to show us that He never deals with us like those guards in the concentration camp. God always has a higher purpose, a greater good for our lives. And in the midst of even the toughest circumstances, He is at work, not just in the circumstances themselves, but in *us*—shaping us as His sons to be more usable and beautiful for Him.

WE ARE A SHOWCASE FOR GLORY
(AND IT'S NOT OURS)

Even in the toughest of circumstances, God's plan is always the same. It's to put His power on display in my life and your life to bring about a greater good—one that will bring Him the glory that only He deserves.

We see this same principle in the New Testament story of a man who was born blind so that the glory of God might be revealed (see John 9:3). Later, that same gospel tells us that God allowed Lazarus to die so that His power might be displayed (see 11:4). These examples show that it is for the greater good of revealing God's glory and power that He is preparing us, sometimes with prolonged suffering. So your life might not make sense right now. But when we each finally see God's larger purpose—and we will!—then you will have the explanation for all your pain.

Dare I say it makes the pain worth it? God will use the sacrifices that He asks or allows you to make, or induces in your life, to shape you for a higher purpose—to bring Himself glory and honor. He will absolutely put His power on display in your life if you persevere.

Where does the power to persevere come from? It comes from the Holy Spirit, but it also comes from accurate knowledge, from having good theology. The good theology and takeaway from this chapter is that God always orchestrates every event in our lives to bring about a greater good. This eternal truth is an essential part of how God makes us into the men He wants us to be. We are never left alone.

As these truths sank in and became part of Joseph's worldview, his purpose became visible and his pain became explainable.

But there's still one more thing. Something else happened to Joseph that God wants to happen to us too.

WHEN PEACE BECOMES POSSIBLE

When Joseph was fifty-six years old, his father died. He took it hard. His brothers took it hard too, in another way. When the funeral was over, they wondered if Joseph held a grudge against them. So they came up with the lie that their father had wanted Joseph to forgive them for their sins and for treating him so badly. What a dysfunctional family!

Who wouldn't understand if Joseph still held his brothers responsible for the pain they inflicted on him forty years earlier? Now that the roles were reversed, he could take his revenge. But when Joseph heard what they said, he wept.

Genesis 50:19–20 records Joseph's response: "Don't be afraid. Am I in the place of God? *You intended to harm me, but God intended it for good* to accomplish what is now being done, the saving of many lives."

Once Joseph understood that his suffering wasn't random, that God's sovereign plan was to use him to save his family and bring God glory, everything changed. His anxiety turned to peace, his bitterness turned to forgiveness, and his desire turned from retaliation to reconciliation. He saw God's larger perspective and purpose, even though it took decades.

You, too, shouldn't be surprised if it takes a long time for you to understand God's larger perspective, but you don't have to wait for decades to find your peace. You can go to school on Joseph.

What Joseph learned the hard way was that God had not abandoned him and that his life was not his own. He saw that he was part of God's bigger picture, and he was able to forgive his brothers and bring reconciliation. Peace became possible when he grasped what God was doing in his life.

Do you see it?

Joseph proves what absolute loyalty to God can do. By putting faithfulness at the top of his list, everything else eventually fell in line. Over time, that same kind of loyalty and faithfulness to God will remake you into the man He had in mind when He created you.

What does this mean to you right now?

THE GREATER GOOD IN THE REALITIES OF LIFE

Let's finish this chapter by applying Joseph's story to four of the biggest recurring challenges men face—marriage, work, health, and money. These are the four areas where most of us will experience our toughest long-term circumstances and problems. So let's see how God employs the principle of a greater good to make men of us in these areas.

Marriage

We'll start with what I believe is the single biggest problem men as a group face today—bigger than all their other problems combined. *Their marriages are not working as God designed.* What can we learn from Joseph that God can use to make us into the husbands He created us to be?

For our marriages, the message is stay the course. Trust that God does have a purpose and that He is always at work in your life and in your relationship.

You may be in a marriage that seems beyond help. I say "seems" because no marriage is beyond the hope of reconstruction by the strong arm of God. Nothing that has happened in your marriage has surprised God. If we learn anything from Joseph, it's that nothing is beyond His redeeming power.

Consider Charles. All Charles did was work. His wife's heart grew stone cold toward him. He retaliated by thinking about how happy he could be with other women and planning a divorce. This went on for a long time. Yet he knew divorce was not God's plan for marriage. Then one day, while he was driving, God supernaturally gave him a deep, unquenchable love for his wife. When he pulled into his driveway, he just sat in his car for a long time, sobbing. And the following week God changed his wife's heart too.

God changed what seemed like irresolvable differences into a greater good—both for them and for others. Today Charles boldly helps other men save their marriages by telling the story of how God intervened in his marriage.

Men routinely ask me how to resolve marriage tensions. A man whose marriage was hanging by a thread asked, "What should I do?"

I asked him, "What do you want to do?"

"I want to make it work!"

"Do you want to be absolutely loyal to God?"

"Yes, more than anything."

Then I said what I always say: "You can't, but Jesus in you can; so put your faith in Him, not what you see, and give it a few years." Give it a few years—that's the school of Joseph talking.

Once I saw a research report claiming that five years after they were divorced, a majority of people wish they would have worked harder to make their marriages work. In fact, an analysis of the National Survey of Families and Households revealed that 86 percent of unhappily married couples who did stick it out found that five years later their marriages were happier.[2]

So if happiness is what you want, stick it out and give it a few more years. Adjust your expectations. Family systems scholar Edwin Friedman stated, "In reality, no human marriage gets a rating of more than 70%."[3] The happiness that working through your problems *will* bring far exceeds the shadow of happiness that divorce *might* bring. Most divorced men I've met have attested that the negative impacts of divorce, especially on their children, seem to go on forever. Besides, you're not the only one whose happiness is at stake. Think in Bible Time.

However, if your wife pulls out anyway, and you are on your own, you can use that time to stand strong and reveal the power and glory of God. You can continue to live in absolute loyalty to Jesus Christ by putting your faith in Him and keeping yourself morally pure until you remarry, or even remarry her. Over a dozen men in our Friday morning Bible study have done just that. Because they stayed true, God brought them back together again with their divorced or separated wives. And it didn't hurt to have a small group of men to meet with on a weekly basis.

Of course, no one can guarantee any specific outcome for your relationship with your wife. What we do learn from Joseph, however, is that you can trust God's Word that nothing has happened to you by human decision—yours or hers—apart from what is permitted by His will. And what God allows He will also use to put His power on display. What God wants from you now is the absolute loyalty that can come only from putting your faith in Jesus Christ. Remain faithful, and God will use your seemingly dead-end marriage to reveal His glory through a greater good. So stay the course.

Work

Another big problem you may face today, if you're like many men, is feeling as if you're stuck in a menial or dead-end job. Your job doesn't line up with who you are. And on top of that, it's going nowhere. That hurts.

But the truths from Joseph's experience can change how you respond to this situation. God can see around the corner to an outcome—to a different job, for example—that you can't. And whatever happens, God is ready to use every day of your life—even today in your unappealing job—for His glory. Look at how God used Joseph's "job" in prison to bring Himself honor and glory.

My brother drives a bus. My brother's peace quotient changed abruptly when he finally realized the truth of Joseph—that nothing could happen to him by human decision apart from God's will. He realized that God must have a purpose for him in driving a bus. And that changed his whole perspective. Now he constantly looks for opportunities to encourage his riders. There are no menial jobs when they are done for the glory of Christ. Every vocation is holy to the Lord.

Health

Nothing will make you feel more abandoned by God than a lingering health problem, whether it's you or a family member who has the problem. It's hard to have joy when you feel crummy. You may have a disability, some kind of long-term illness, or an alcohol or drug problem. You may be walking around with a health issue that leaves you feeling hopeless, feeling that nothing will ever work out right in your life because of it.

But that's not true. God will use your health issue, as tough as it is, for a greater good.

Money

A fourth problem is money. You may have been upside down financially for so long that you've lost hope. Sometimes you feel like you are on top of the mountain, and sometimes you feel like the mountain is on top of you.

Don't give up. Believe the gospel. God is sovereignly orchestrating your life. Nothing done to you by human decision can ever be done apart from God's will. Whatever others have meant for evil, He will use it for good.

Always remember this: Joseph carried his pain for over two decades until God revealed the liberating truth that nothing can happen to us by human decision apart from His knowledge and father-like concern. That's what the Bible says. Not even one sparrow can fall to the ground apart from His will.

What have you been carrying around, and for how long? Whatever it is, God wants you to know that He is making you into part of His larger plan to redeem this world and bring glory to His name. That's who you are.

Trust Him and wait for Him, and in due time
- your purpose will become visible
- your pain will become explainable
- your peace will become possible

Why? Because God makes men by orchestrating even the toughest circumstances of our lives for a greater good.

For Reflection and Discussion

1. Do you have a marriage, work, health, money, or other major long-term problem that you pray and pray about but nothing seems to change? How does it make you feel abandoned by God?

2. What was the liberating principle that God revealed to Joseph and, through Joseph, to us? Does that change your perspective, and if so, how?

3. What did you need to learn or be reminded of in this chapter? How do you think that will help you make better sense of your life and become more of the man God created you to be?

3

MOSES

THE PRINCIPLE
OF PERSONAL
TRANSFORMATION

HOW GOD CHANGES
A MAN'S CHARACTER

Twenty-five years ago God told one of my best friends, Rick, "Disciple young men so that they can go and disciple others." Ten years ago God led another friend, Dennis, to start a used-car dealership to advance Christian principles in business and help fund kingdom work.

God is like that. He gives us callings and missions to accomplish important things. But often those callings don't go the way we think they will. Far from it. Dennis had to close his dealership during the great recession.

Who among us hasn't felt led by God to do something that we thought was important but ended up with egg on our face?

Maybe you felt called to a career that required special training or education, but after many years it still hasn't come together.

Maybe you always knew you were meant to start a business for yourself. You threw yourself into it with great anticipation. Now it's Friday and you have no idea how you're going to make payroll.

Or maybe you had a dream of becoming a cycle breaker, putting an end to the pattern of dysfunction in your family history. You thought you would become a godly husband with a picture-perfect marriage and model children. But it's turning out to be so much harder than you thought.

You took a big leap of faith—and accepted a lot of risk—to follow and serve God. But based on how things appear to be working out, you wonder, *Was this really from God, or did I just make this up in my own imagination?* You still love Him, but you feel confused and discouraged.

Here's the problem. God has an agenda, but we universally come into the Christian faith with our own agendas. And it takes a while to get on the same agenda with God.

So how does God get us on His agenda? He enrolls us in Character College to open our eyes and change the way we see the world. Here's a sentence that captures the full principle:

> God makes men by taking us through
> a humbling process that fundamentally
> changes the way we think.

No man illustrates this principle better than Moses. In this chapter we're going to follow Moses's quest to do something great for God, see how it backfired, walk with him through the prolonged wilderness experience that followed, and then figure out how God used all that to forge him into a man who made a truly epic difference—the one man who towers over Jewish history like no other.

In the process, you'll see how God takes our flawed efforts and wilderness experiences and lovingly molds us into men who can accomplish that noble dream He has for each and every man.

BORN SPECIAL, THEN WHAT?

In Egypt, a pharaoh rose to power who had never heard of Joseph's success, and he started oppressing the Israelites. He was so evil that he forced the Israelites to throw out their newborn babies so they would die. Think of it as live-birth abortion.

Acts 7:20 says, "At that time Moses was born, and he was no ordinary child."

His family hid him and cared for him for three months. When they couldn't hide him any longer, his mother coated a small basket with tar and pitch. She then placed Moses in the basket and "put it among the reeds along the bank of the Nile" (Exodus 2:3).

When Pharaoh's daughter went down to the river to bathe, she saw the basket, opened it, and found little Moses crying. Moved, she took the baby and raised him as her own. In an amazing plot twist, the Israelite who was supposed to die at birth was now Egyptian royalty—growing up in the halls of power, educated in all the wisdom of the pharaohs. His opportunities were unlimited, and he rose to them, developing all the talents, skills, and aptitudes that God had given him.

Life must have been good. He was royalty—a Prince William. Yet he knew he was adopted. Scripture says, "When Moses was forty years old, he decided to visit his fellow Israelites" (Acts 7:23).

He knew he was a Hebrew. And he saw his own people straining under the heavy burden of slavery and forced labor. During his visit, "he saw one of them [a fellow Hebrew] being mistreated by an Egyptian, so he went to his defense and avenged him by killing the Egyptian" (verse 24).

But there's more.

> The next day Moses came upon two Israelites who were fighting. He tried to reconcile them by saying, "Men, you are brothers; why do you want to hurt each other?"
>
> But the man who was mistreating the other pushed Moses aside and said, "Who made you ruler and judge over us? Do you want to kill me as you killed the Egyptian yesterday?" (verses 26–28)

Moses was convinced he was the right man doing the right thing for God. And he assumed his people would see it too. "Moses thought that his own people would realize that God was using him to rescue them, but they did not" (verse 25).

Moses had a vision that he was going to be the deliverer of his people. That was his noble dream. But when he went out to execute that dream—and even killed a man to try to make it happen—he was rejected and failed.

All of us know that kind of disappointment and confusion at some level, don't we?

Here's the problem. Moses wasn't ready to do what he had been

called to do. His character wasn't deep enough to support his calling—
at least not yet. Moses needed a makeover. He needed a different way
of looking at the world. He needed a new worldview.

To make matters even worse, Pharaoh heard about the Egyptian's
death and tried to kill Moses. So Moses fled to the parched land of
Midian and settled there as a foreigner. It's interesting. Moses had
thought God was going to use him powerfully to bring about a great
deliverance. Instead, he had to flee for his life into a place that was
definitely not flowing with milk and honey.

Why did God put Moses in a position to lead and then let him
fail? And for us, why does God give us dreams, visions, and desires that
end up in failure and frustration? For example, when my friend Rick
went out to disciple young men, he couldn't get any to join him—
at least not right away. And I already mentioned what happened to
Dennis.

Of course, we can't answer that question for every situation, but
we do know what was going on with Moses. Looking back, we can see
how God used those early failures of Moses to shape him more fully
into the man he was created to be. And through his story we can learn
some truths about how God wants to humble us and prepare our "inner man" for future service.

HE WENT BEFORE HE WAS SENT

God had given Moses a desire to rescue his people, but then overcon-
fidence led him to get ahead of God. He went before he was sent. As a
result, he failed. His timing was off. His pride got him in big trouble.

Most of us can relate to Moses, can't we? Haven't we all hit the accelerator before we got the green light? Even though we feel drawn by God to do something or go somewhere, we can easily leap into action before He sends us. What happens next is usually a lot of pain and regret.

Out there in the desert, reflecting on his leadership fiasco, it must have seemed to Moses that he had permanently blown it. That he would never be heard from again and would die in obscurity.

Why would God call men like Moses and you and me to rise to a noble task only to let us fall flat on our faces?

Fortunately, we have the advantage of hindsight. As I read the story, it seems obvious that there was too much Moses in Moses. His motives—at least some of them—were admirable. But I'd say his judgment and character weren't up to the demands of leadership. At least not yet. (Leaders with the character to lead a great nation, for example, don't generally think murder is a smart first move.) Clearly, he was acting in his own wisdom and strength, not under the inspiration of the Holy Spirit.

As a result, there were things God wanted to work *into* the character of Moses, and there were things He wanted to work *out* of his character, and those things take time—Bible Time. God enrolled Moses in the Wilderness Branch of Character College for a postgraduate course in personal transformation to fundamentally change the way he thought.

It's the same with us. You see, we tend to be interested in the success of our *circumstances*—career, family, and even our good works, such as feeding hungry schoolchildren or volunteering for a youth ministry or bringing clean water to a poverty-stricken village. But God is more interested in the success of our character than the success of our circumstances.

That's not to say God doesn't want us to be successful in our circumstances. He does. But even more than that, He wants to forge our character so we can be faithful stewards who act in a way that's worthy of our circumstances.

God will never sacrifice our character to improve our circumstances. He simply loves us too much to let us destroy ourselves. Like Moses, and probably you too, I learned this the hard way.

MOLASSES SWAMP

For the first dozen years of my spiritual journey, I believed in Jesus but pretty much did what I wanted to do. At first I didn't know that Jesus wanted to be involved in all the details of my life—freshman mistake. But then, when I finally began to understand that He did, I still wanted to call the shots—sophomore mistake.

Like Moses, I had a vision of being a deliverer. I pictured myself becoming the first person in my family ever to get a college degree. I pictured myself becoming a wildly successful businessman and provider. I saw myself as a cycle breaker delivering my family from repeating the mistakes of my failed youth. I was sure that God had "sent" me to do all these things. But as a practical matter, while my intentions were noble, my worldview was really one of selfish ambition, not humble surrender.

One day it dawned on me that some of the other Christian guys around me were getting very different—and enviable—results from their faith. So I called a time-out and decided to study the Bible to see if I could figure out what was going on. I thought that after a couple of weeks I would get it all sorted out, make the fix, and then really go and do something great for God.

But when God finally had my attention, it was like I had run into a giant swamp of refrigerated molasses. I couldn't move. For the next two and a half years I tried my best to get out of it, but I was stuck. Yet something more important was happening. All during that time, I was reading God's Word, and He was speaking to my heart. He started working some things into my character—and working some things out of my character too. A transformation had begun.

At the time, I was so overconfident and prideful that I thought once I was "fixed," the new, revised version of me could grow my business bigger and better than ever. But as I said, God is more interested in shaping our character than in improving our circumstances. And that takes time.

Also at that time, I was having debilitating headaches—mainly from the stress of trying to do more than I was created to do. One day I was reading 1 Peter 4:1: "Since Christ suffered in his body, arm yourselves also with the same attitude, because he who has suffered in his body is done with sin." Did you hear that? When the body suffers, sin loses power.

The text continues, "As a result, he does not live the rest of his earthly life for evil human desires, but rather for the will of God" (verse 2). Yes, the wilderness experience is painful, but God uses the pain like a can opener to get inside our hearts and open us up to the transforming power of His Spirit.

After reading these verses, I opened the front flap of the Bible my wife and kids gave me and wrote, "I want to live the rest of my earthly life for the will of God. 1 Peter 4:1–2." I really meant it. Still do!

However, I was an immature believer, like Moses. Because I was an underequipped and, hence, overconfident Christian, I was thinking,

Wow! Now that I've really surrendered my life to God, just imagine how much He can do with me on His side. What a trophy. Lucky God.

I wonder if that's how Moses felt when he went out prematurely to rescue his own people.

In my naiveté I thought my surrender to the will of God meant that I had hit rock bottom. I thought that special day would mark the beginning of doing something great for God. And in a way, it did. But first God said, "Okay, now that I have your attention, I have some important things to teach you that you haven't been willing to hear. So let's get started." Apparently, there was still too much Pat in Pat.

So instead of bringing me out of the wilderness, He drove me further in. Over the next few months, my business was decimated. God leveled me right down to the foundation.

Thank God I had the right foundation, though. The Bible says no one can lay any foundation except Christ (see 1 Corinthians 3:11). So I had the right foundation, but I had not been building on it in the right way. I'd been building with wood, hay, and stubble. When I wrote that declaration of surrender in my Bible, it's as though God said, "I really think you're serious, Pat. The problem is you've given Me so little to work with that I'm going to have to start over with you."

That's because, like Moses, I had taken matters into my own hands. I didn't wait for the Lord to lead me. Instead, I was building a business and life based on my own best thinking and ambitions. Essentially, I went before I was sent. God needed to humble me because I wasn't strong enough to humble myself.

Men, if I had actually caught what I was chasing, I am almost certain that today I would be divorced, alienated from my children, filthy rich, eaten up with pride, mean as a snake, and bitter at the world. But what at the time looked like God letting me down was God saving my life. It's the same for all of us. It's a perspective—one we learn by going through the humbling wilderness process we're talking about in this chapter.

While this was happening, I could tell what my friends were thinking: *Wow, he must have really ticked God off.*

I wanted to say, "You don't understand. This is not a curse. This is a blessing!" I had gotten to a point where I hated my life. I had everything I ever wanted in terms of money, influence, and reputation, yet I was miserable. But when God started removing the things I had been so sure would make me happy, I felt unshackled from the chains of idolatry, materialism, and worldliness. I can't help but wonder if Moses felt that way.

My friends thought I was cursed because they were looking at my circumstances. God was grinding me up, yes, but He was also remaking my character—transforming me more into the image of His Son, Jesus. I'm guessing you know what I am talking about, because most men I know who have set out to follow God have been through this.

What can you do if you're in the wilderness right now because you went before you were sent?

One thing you most definitely *don't* want to do is try to shorten the duration of your wilderness experience. As I said, a major reason God puts us there in the first place is to work some things *into* and *out of* our character. If we don't go *through* it, then we won't learn everything He has for us *in* it. You'll never grow in faith if you keep dropping the This Is How You Grow class.

So instead of praying that God will shorten the duration of your hard times, pray that you will learn everything God has for you during your wilderness experience so that you won't have to travel that road again.

What clues do we find in Moses's life about how God goes about changing our character? Let's dive further into his story.

HIS STUMBLE MADE HIM HUMBLE

Forty years later we find a much different Moses about to graduate from the Midian campus of Character College. Gone was the proud, overconfident man who once thought he could single-handedly deliver his people. His stumble had made him humble.

Humbling hurts. The names Moses gave his two sons tell us a lot about how painful it can be. Moses named his first son Gershom because, he said, "I have become an alien in a foreign land" (Exodus 18:3). Have you been overseas in a foreign land where people don't look like you and no one can understand a word you say? Suddenly it occurs to you, *What if I had a heart attack or got hit by a car? What would I do?* It's a helpless feeling to be an alien, and that's exactly how Moses felt.

Moses named his other son Eliezer because, he said, "My father's God was my helper; he saved me from the sword of Pharaoh" (verse 4). Notice that he said "my *father's* God." I think Moses was so discouraged and felt like God was so far away that he couldn't even call Him "*my* God."

Later, when Moses *did* become the deliverer of his people, the Bible account says this of him: "Now Moses was a very humble man, more humble than anyone else on the face of the earth" (Numbers 12:3). Talk about turning a one-eighty!

The wilderness had radically changed him.

In my late thirties and early forties, I went through a nine-year wilderness experience that I thought would never end. Forty years? To me, that is unimaginable. But Moses didn't become the man God had in mind overnight, and neither will we. I've found that the process of transformation and learning humility often goes like this:

Step 1: I tell God what I'm going to do.

Step 2: God responds.

Step 3: I beg God to let me do it anyway.

Step 4: He humbles me until I listen.

Step 5: God tells me what He is going to do.

Think about where you are right now in this sequence. Are you somewhere in the first three stages—proudly doing all the talking and trying to call the shots? Or has a wilderness experience humbled you, and now you find yourself ready to listen? Humbling us so we can hear Him is one of the main ways God transforms men's lives.

As you'll see next, true humility before God nearly always precedes what we wanted so much in the first place—a real, God-timed, and God-sized opportunity.

Let me show you what I mean.

A Push from a Burning Bush

Moses went before he was sent, and his stumble made him humble. In his remedial classes at Character College he was tested, transformed, and made ready to be sent to serve God. And that's when he got a push from a burning bush.

No doubt the last thing Moses expected after four decades in the Midian outback was a personal encounter with God. But that's exactly what he got. One day he was taking care of his father-in-law's sheep when he saw a bush in flames. Strangely, though, the bush was not burning up. Puzzled and a little afraid, he walked closer to investigate. At that moment he heard the Lord calling his name: "Moses! Moses!" (Exodus 3:4). You see, no matter how things had felt to Moses over the last forty years, God had not abandoned him.

God is never more near than when He seems far away. God had been with Moses the entire time, rightsizing him for his future. What Moses no doubt thought was abandonment was actually equipping. In fact, it's easy to mistake equipping as abandonment, isn't it?

During all those hot, lonely years, God had been molding Moses to be more patient, persistent, hardworking, and wily—a proven back-country survivor. Equipping him, in other words, for a great task. I think it's obvious that God sent him *into* the wilderness to equip him so later he could deliver his people *through* the wilderness—a mission that would also take forty years. But of course Moses didn't know that at the time.

In the same way, I honestly believe God is equipping Dennis— my friend who lost his used-car dealership—for a great task with a great trial. All of us, really, are going to get a push from a burning bush.

GRADUATION DAY

How did Moses respond to God's voice in the burning bush? He said humbly, "Here I am" (Exodus 3:4). There was no angry outburst. No barrage of questions. No proud "This is what I'll do for You, God." No "Why did You do this to me?"

Simply, "Here I am."

God replied, "I am the God of your fathers, the God of Abraham,

Isaac and Jacob.... Take off your sandals; the place where you are standing is holy ground" (Acts 7:32–33). As you can imagine, Moses shook with fear.

Then the Lord let him in on the big picture: "I have indeed seen the oppression of my people in Egypt. I have heard their groaning and have come down to set them free. Now come, I will send you back to Egypt" (verse 34).

But *that* seemed entirely too much for Moses. He had become a silhouette of the forty-year-old man who long ago had so confidently taken God's business into his own hands. Gone was the self-assurance. Repeatedly, Moses tried to explain to God why he was *not* adequate for the job. "Who am I to go?" "Who should I say sent me?" "What if they don't believe me?" "But I'm not a good speaker, and I stutter." "Oh, Lord, please send someone else."

It's interesting. When Moses considered himself adequate to deliver his people, God considered him inadequate. But decades later and a world away, when Moses considered himself inadequate, God considered him exactly right for the job. He passed his final exam. He graduated. He was transformed into a different kind of man—a humble man ready to live in utter dependence on the Lord.

Men, God does His best work when we do our best work. But it's equally true that we can't do our best work until we have been tutored by the Principal of the principle we've been exploring in this chapter.

A transformation takes place when we are humbled that we can't get any other way. It's a major principle in how God makes men. I think the lesson is clear. God can use an inadequate man once he realizes he is inadequate.

After that, graduation.

YOU ARE NO ORDINARY
CHILD EITHER

Moses was no ordinary child partly because no child is ordinary. The fact that you were born at all makes you remarkable, since you're the product of one out of hundreds of millions of spermatozoa that competed to fertilize a single egg in your mother's womb. As David prayed in Psalm 139:13, 16,

> You created my inmost being;
>> you knit me together in my mother's womb....
>> Your eyes saw my unformed body.
> All the days ordained for me
>> were written in your book
>> before one of them came to be.

Bottom line? Your life is also a spiritual phenomenon. You are one of God's crowning achievements. You are the full expression of His creative genius—and no troubled marriage or disastrous employment record or sin-dogged season on your part can possibly change this fact. God was at His very best when He made you.

Like Moses, you are no ordinary child.

However, as it was with Moses, every one of us starts our spiritual journey with a worldview that needs a makeover. Where are you in this makeover process?

Perhaps, like me, you went before you were sent and ended up with egg on your face. Or maybe you have held back, waiting for a sign. In any event, you're pretty sure God has sidelined you for a

season. If so, don't try to short-circuit a process that God has designed
to prepare and equip you for His service.

Maybe you've already seen a burning bush and have experienced
a personal transformation. Or maybe you have been humbled but are
still passing time in the wilderness, waiting for that burning-bush experience when God will restore you to His service. Remember, God is
never more near than when He seems far away. Wait upon the Lord.
Think Bible Time. The purpose of the wilderness is for God to recali-
brate how we see Him, ourselves, and our role in the world.

For Reflection and Discussion

1. Have you ever felt called by God to do something important
   but ended up with egg on your face? If so, what happened?
2. In this chapter we saw what happened to Moses when he tried
   to do something important for God, how it backfired, the
   long period when he felt confused and abandoned by God, his
   prolonged wilderness experience, and how God used all that to
   forge him into a man He could use to do something that really
   made a difference. Have you experienced a similar pattern, and
   if so, where are you in that process now? Explain your answer.
3. Does the story of Moses help you understand that God is taking you through a humbling process that will fundamentally
   change the way you think? Why do you think the wilderness
   experience is so central to personal transformation and change
   in your own life?

4

GIDEON

THE PRINCIPLE OF THE UNEXPECTED LEADER

How God Turns a Man's Fear and Weakness into Strength

In 2011 the leadership team at Man in the Mirror—the men's discipleship ministry I founded—sensed the Lord leading us to undertake a huge project to hire 330 full-time area directors in local comunities to help churches more effectively disciple men. To put that in perspective, we made the decision when we had only fifteen full-time staff!

We are now deep in the middle of this project. And as you might imagine, it is harder than we thought and is taking longer than we expected. Frankly, we know there's no way to succeed unless God is in it.

Has God presented you with a calling, task, or mission so daunting that it raises all kinds of doubts and fears? Maybe you heard,

- "You're going to be a father." And you thought, *I don't know how to do this.*
- "I want you to take on this project." And you thought, *But I've never done that.*
- "We really need you to be a small-group leader." And you thought, *But I don't know how to lead a group.*
- "You're being promoted to floor manager." And you thought, *But I've never managed people before.*

You probably already know this, but God doesn't seem to mind teaching His disciples how to swim by throwing us into the deep end of the pool. He doesn't mind tapping us for tasks that are way beyond our depth. Sometimes He prepares us for the mission—as He did with Joseph and Moses. But then there are other times when we feel we are in way over our heads and God says, "You're up. You're My pick."

What you may not have realized before is that these nerve-racking times are one of God's favorite ways to mold us into the unexpected leaders for Him that we never thought we could be—maybe never even wanted to be.

In this chapter you're going to meet a man like that. A man who—as far as we know—never aspired to anything. In fact, he tried to get out of serving God. He was having enough trouble just making ends meet from day to day. He certainly wasn't anyone's pick for "hero of the year." But God saw something in him that he didn't see in himself.

By reading this man's story, you'll find out that what happened to him can also happen to us. And you'll see how God can use you way beyond your obvious capabilities and in spite of your fear. You'll see how God actually turns our fear and weakness into strength so dramatically that it would be crazy for us to take any credit. The principle for this chapter is,

> God makes men by turning our weakness
> into strength in such a striking way that
> only He can get the glory.

THE RELUCTANT LIBERATOR

It was a harsh, brutal time. Israel had worshiped other gods, so God had allowed the Midianites to raid their crops and destroy their food supply. Some people even had to flee from their homes to hide in caves. Midian ravaged and impoverished the land for seven years until the Israelites cried out to God for help.

And as God does when people turn back to Him in humble prayer, He decided to send them a man. But he was not the man you might expect. God didn't pick a powerful leader from the existing political structure, a pedigreed man from one of the city's first families, a recognized holy man, a great warrior from the military, or a rising star in the business community. Instead, He chose just about the most unexpected man possible. God turned to a man by the name of Gideon.

When we first learn about Gideon, he was living like a refugee in his own home. In desperation, he had turned a winepress into a hideout where he could prepare food for his family without its getting confiscated by the enemy. And then it happened. The Bible says,

> The angel of the LORD came and sat down under the oak in
> Ophrah that belonged to Joash the Abiezrite, where his son

Gideon was threshing wheat in a winepress to keep it from the
Midianites. When the angel of the LORD appeared to Gideon,
he said, "The LORD is with you, mighty warrior." (Judges
6:11–12)

As you will soon see, Gideon was maybe the most unlikely man
in the entire Bible to be a "mighty warrior" and lead an army. And
Gideon would have agreed with that assessment! Never has there been
a more reluctant, confidence-lacking, fear-filled leader. If you and I
were called on to pick a leader, a man like Gideon would never even
cross our minds.

What was God thinking? God didn't see the present Gideon. God
saw the future Gideon—the Gideon who would become the man
God had created him to be. And here is the secret: We see ourselves as
we are, but God sees us as we are going to be.

Yet all Gideon could see was an insurmountable list of problems
and obstacles—the same ones that had sent him into hiding in the
first place. The first words from Gideon's mouth recorded in the Bible
were a barrage of fearful questions draped in doubt:

"But sir," Gideon replied [to the angel], "if the LORD is with us,
why has all this happened to us? Where are all his wonders that
our fathers told us about when they said, 'Did not the LORD
bring us up out of Egypt?' But now the LORD has abandoned
us and put us into the hand of Midian." (verse 13)

Haven't we all asked those kinds of questions and had similar
doubts and fears many times? And when our worldview is limited to

what we can see and our own power and strength, those questions make all the sense in the world.

So how did God respond to Gideon's questions and doubts—and the charge that the Lord had abandoned them? And moreover, how will He respond to us?

A MAJORITY OF TWO

One amazing thing about how God makes men is that He doesn't argue with anybody. Instead of explaining or defending Himself, God simply gave Gideon his marching orders: "The LORD turned to him and said, 'Go in the strength you have and save Israel out of Midian's hand. Am I not sending you?'" (verse 14).

God never really addressed Gideon's questions. And as we'll see in chapter 8, He didn't answer Job's questions about why he had suffered either. Likewise, it's highly improbable that God will answer you when you ask, "Why, God?" Instead, He simply tells you what He wants you to do. You are the one God is choosing to change the world.

But Gideon knew too much about himself. He just couldn't get his mind around what God was telling him to do: "'But Lord,' Gideon asked, 'how can I save Israel? My clan is the weakest in Manasseh, and I am the least in my family'" (verse 15).

Gideon didn't think he could get the job done, and that wasn't misplaced fear or false modesty. He really wasn't a likely guy to lead a sophisticated military operation. But God decided to use the weakest man from the weakest clan so there would be no confusion about who was doing the delivering.

Even so, God still needed to calm the frayed nerves of Gideon so he would agree to step out in faith. So God told him simply, "I will be with you" (verse 16).

Ah, there it is. "I will be with you."

That's what God wants you to hear too. No matter how overwhelming and terrifying God's calling on your life may appear, He wants you to know, "I will be with you." Whether it's a calling to adopt an international child, step into the culture wars, or say no to a boss who asks you to cheat, God wants you to know that He will be right there with you.

You may feel you are the weakest man or the most unlikely person—and you might be right. You might be the most reluctant person in the world to do the assignment God gives you to do. But it doesn't make any difference if God is with you. God and you constitute a majority in any situation.

Then God did something for Gideon that He doesn't always do. He promised a specific outcome: "The LORD said to him, 'I will be with you. And you will destroy the Midianites as if you were fighting against one man'" (verse 16, NLT).

But even with that assurance, Gideon was still hesitant.

How Can I Be Sure?

Haven't we all, like Gideon, thought the Holy Spirit was speaking to our hearts, but still we weren't 100 percent sure? We wondered, *Is that really You, Lord?*

At this point in Gideon's story, it would be nice and tidy if he simply accepted God's promise and marched out to do battle. But if he had, then we probably wouldn't be able to relate to him very well, would we? So instead, the Lord lets us see that He allowed a doubt-plagued Gideon to ask Him for a sign, something that would boost his confidence: "If now I have found favor in your eyes, give me a sign that it is really you talking to me" (verse 17).

And God graciously did exactly that. So Gideon sent out a call to arms, and men throughout his clan responded, bolstering his courage. Sometimes a small step is needed to give us enough confidence to take a big step.

But even then Gideon still had doubts. So he put out the famous fleece questions. He said to God,

> If you will save Israel by my hand as you have promised—look,
> I will place a wool fleece on the threshing floor. If there is dew
> only on the fleece and all the ground is dry, then I will know
> that you will save Israel by my hand, as you said. (verses 36–37)

And it happened just like he asked.

> Then Gideon said to God, "Do not be angry with me. Let me
> make just one more request. Allow me one more test with the
> fleece. This time make the fleece dry and the ground covered
> with dew." (verse 39)

And it happened again just as he asked.

What a gracious God! Finally this reluctant man began to feel the butterflies starting to settle down. Finally his doubts started to give way to faith in the unexpected call God had placed on his life—the call to be a leader.

Gideon had said, "I could never do that."

God responded, "Yes, you can, because I will be with you."

Have you thought asking for a sign would be irreverent or show a lack of faith? You shouldn't. God gave us the story of Gideon as an example of how God makes men. The message is clear. If you need a sign because you are reluctant or fearful, God is not opposed to giving you some encouragement along the way.

God's sign or confirmation to you may or may not be as dramatic as Gideon's. He may speak to you through a friend's advice, by quickening a verse in the Bible to your heart, through a job offer in another city that comes through (or falls through), or by letting you keep your job even though you told your boss you wouldn't lie for him. Or it could be as simple as the Holy Spirit quietly whispering to your spirit, "I am with you." Silence is a sign too—one that means "no" or "wait."

So if you need a sign, ask. It is the regular practice of God to confirm what He wants us to do. In fact, guidance is one of the main roles of the Holy Spirit. Jesus put it like this: "The Counselor, the Holy Spirit, whom the Father will send in my name, will teach you all things and will remind you of everything I have said to you" (John 14:26).

How Did It Turn Out?

With multiple assurances in hand, Gideon assembled 32,000 troops to attack an enemy force of 135,000 soldiers. Even though he was outnumbered four to one, you won't believe what happened next! "The LORD said to Gideon, 'You have too many men for me to deliver Midian into their hands'" (Judges 7:2).

Gideon must have been thinking God was not very good at

math. The Lord continued, *"In order that Israel may not boast against me that her own strength has saved her,* announce now to the people, 'Anyone who trembles with fear may turn back and leave Mount Gilead'" (verses 2–3).

And there it is. God didn't want the strongest, most powerful man—or army—to lead. He wanted His people to realize that it was the power of God, and not their own strength, that was saving their nation. "So twenty-two thousand men left, while ten thousand remained" (verse 3).

Now the odds against them were more than thirteen to one! In what must have seemed like an absurdity to Gideon, the Lord then said, "There are still too many men" (verse 4). Eventually God reduced the fighting forces down to a mere three hundred men—the famous "Gideon's 300." Then He said to Gideon, "With the three hundred men... I will save you and give the Midianites into your hands" (verse 7).

So the weakest man in the weakest clan, the reluctant leader who questioned God, the fear-filled one to whom the Lord said, "I will be with you," the man who needed several signs was now reduced to leading a fighting force of a mere three hundred men. And finally the Lord was ready to use him for His glory. The odds at that point no longer mattered because victory by their own strength was completely out of the question. Victory was impossible without divine intervention.

What happened next flabbergasted the world, both then and now. With a tiny force of three hundred men, Gideon's carefully choreographed attack threw 135,000 Midianites into panic and mass hysteria. Those who didn't kill each other fled the camp. It must have looked like Saddam Hussein's army retreating along the infamous Highway of Death during Desert Storm.

At that point Gideon reassembled his larger army and gave pursuit. In the ensuing battle Gideon achieved a dominating victory. The Midianite army was completely routed but—don't miss God's plan—in such an improbable way that only God could get the glory.

So why did God include the inspiring account of Gideon and the odd circumstances of his victory in the Bible? Simply this: Our weakness is the ideal medium for God to display His power and presence. Gideon accomplished an incredible task, and the big idea is that you can too.

Let's explore this further.

God Is Not Limited by Our Weakness

Weakness comes in many forms. But God is not limited by your weakness. God wants you to know that, because He is strong, it doesn't matter if you are weak.

When God called me from real estate to ministry, I didn't really know what I was supposed to do. I was not a reluctant leader, but I certainly was not some big prize for God. So I began to pray. The only thing I ever sensed out of those prayers was the word *Jackson*. That was my "sign." I figured it must be Jackson, Mississippi, because I had been there a couple of times to speak at men's gatherings when I was still in business.

I knew two men in Jackson fairly well—a pastor and a layman. So I called them. They were both excited that I wanted to come and minister in Jackson. I wondered if I was going to be the next Billy Graham, so I proposed a plan for a citywide outreach event.

However, when I went there to meet with a planning group of

pastors and leaders, they said, "That's great, but evangelism is not our problem. Our problem is that half of Jackson is white, half of Jackson is black, and we do not know each other. Our greatest need is for racial reconciliation."

I felt electricity. Over the previous eighteen years, Tom Skinner and I had become best friends. Tom, an African American, was already in ministry. I wondered if Tom would be interested in a joint ministry venture with his Caucasian buddy. So I placed a call to him right there in the conference room with those leaders. I asked him if he would come to explore what we could do together to address racial reconciliation in Jackson. He agreed. We eventually concluded that, since God had made such a big investment in our relationship, this was a way He could get a return on His investment.

Our first citywide meeting in Jackson was a kickoff luncheon with about eighty pastors and leaders in attendance. After the meeting, one of the pastors came up to me and said, "This is very exciting that you are here, because I'm part of a group of pastors who have been praying for years that God would send a man to help us heal our city. But I'm a little surprised that He sent you. In fact, you remind me of the verse that talks about how God will use the weak things of this world."

I think he had the gift of discouragement. But he was right.

Brothers, think of what you were when you were called. Not many of you were wise by human standards; not many were influential; not many were of noble birth. But God chose the foolish things of the world to shame the wise; God chose the weak things of the world to shame the strong. He chose the lowly things of this world and the despised things—and the things that are not—to nullify the things that are, so that no one may boast before him. (1 Corinthians 1:26–29)

God does use the weak things of this world. He takes one man with not much to offer, but a willingness to offer it, and makes something from that. I once heard a preacher say, "God works through the present and willing, not the absent and able."

Together, the pastors and leaders in Jackson, Tom, and I helped start Mission Mississippi, a ministry of racial reconciliation. But just as with Gideon, those afraid of racial reconciliation dropped out until we were left with Gideon's 300. Yet God was not limited by our weakness. On the contrary, His power shone all the brighter because of our weakness. I was there only for the start, but today Mission Mississippi has chapters in over twenty cities throughout Mississippi and has become a model for the nation. And it was born out of Gideon-like weakness.

Is there something that God has put on your heart to do? You may be the weakest man in the weakest clan, but if you are willing to offer yourself, He will use you. He will be with you, He will give the victory, and He will probably do it in such a striking way that it will be impossible for you to say you did it yourself—as He did with me. That is the first lesson from the life of Gideon. God is not limited by our weakness.

In fact, God turns our weakness into strength.

STRENGTH IS FOUND IN WEAKNESS

Chuck Colson went to prison for his role in the Watergate scandal. Through that crisis, Colson became a Christian. After his release, he founded Prison Fellowship, a profoundly successful prison ministry. Out of all of Colson's substantial accomplishments—special counsel to the president of the United States, marine, attorney—isn't it ironic that God would choose the only thing at which he ever really failed to become the foundation of his ministry? But that's often how God works.

God routinely takes our failures and weaknesses—those things that make us vulnerable—and turns them into strengths. In other words, you might be a strong decision maker and leader, but God is more likely to take a moral failure and give you a ministry in that area instead.

My wife and I are friends with two couples who experienced profound pain and separation but who, by God's grace, were able to restore their marriages. Out of that brokenness, God gave them a ministry to other hurting couples. Like attracts like, and they can relate to the pain of broken couples because they've been there.

Maybe you have a son with AIDS, and because of that you have been able to lead other young men with AIDS to Jesus Christ. Or maybe you grew up in a home where you did not learn about biblical manhood, so your passion, like mine, is men's discipleship—to see men become godly leaders, husbands, and fathers. Or maybe you're a recovering alcoholic to whom God has given a burden for other alcoholics.

God is far more likely to give you a ministry out of your weakness than to give you a ministry out of your strength. In fact, God turns weakness *into* strength—His strength. Jesus put it this way: "My grace is all you need. My power works best in weakness" (2 Corinthians 12:9, NLT).

How, practically, does Christ's power work best in weakness? For that answer, there's another point to take from Gideon.

IDENTIFY WHAT YOU'RE DOING WITH GOD

When Gideon went out to meet the vast Midianite army with a mere three hundred men, one thing was clear. He had no illusion of success apart from a miraculous victory from God.

So what was his secret? How did he succeed? Gideon so closely identified what he was doing with God that before his enemies could prevail against him, they would first have to prevail against God. Listen to what he said:

> Get up! For the LORD has given you victory over the Midianite hordes!…
>
> As soon as I and those with me blow the ram's horns, blow your horns, too, all around the entire camp, and shout, "For the LORD and for Gideon!" (Judges 7:15, 18, NLT)

And what was the result? "Each man stood at his position around the camp and watched as all the Midianites rushed around in a panic, shouting as they ran to escape" (verse 21, NLT). God threw them into such confusion that they started killing each other while Gideon stood watching.

The message is clear. If you're feeling the hot breath of imminent defeat, you still have a card to play. Imitate Gideon. Even though he faced such overwhelming odds, he won by declaring that the battle was the Lord's. Once you know what God wants you to do, so closely identify everything you're doing with the Lord that before others can prevail against you, they must first prevail against God.

Always remember, it does not make any difference if you are the weakest, most inadequate, most deeply flawed man who ever walked the face of the planet. When God says, "I will be with you," that means He will show His greatness through you despite your fears, shortcomings, and weaknesses.

YOUR INVITATION TO BECOME AN UNEXPECTED LEADER

Frankly, no one ever told me I could be a leader. That just wasn't a part of the conversations in my home or schools growing up. But God had a different plan for my life. A Gideon plan. An unexpected plan.

After I became a Christian, God started giving me leadership assignments. But I always felt uncomfortable being called a leader. In fact, I deflected all such references, even as God was giving me more and more leadership responsibilities as a man, husband, father, disciple maker, churchman, business owner, and citizen.

It wasn't until I was roughly forty-five years old that I finally became comfortable with people calling me a leader. So if you feel you are the weakest man from the weakest clan, I can relate. And if you *still* feel that way, I can tell you that your journey is far from over.

Your transformation probably won't happen overnight. But day by day, year by year, God plans to turn each of us into His unexpected leaders—men who will reclaim some small part of this world in such a striking way that *only* He can get the glory.

And here's something you don't want to miss. Even if you *never* become strong, God will still use you, because He takes great pleasure in using the weak things of this world. That's what makes us so unexpected. Will you join me? If God is for us, who can be against us?

For Reflection and Discussion

1. If applicable, what has God called you to do that you have been reluctant or felt inadequate to pursue, and why?

2. Has anyone ever told you, "You're a leader"? Describe the impact that hearing, or not hearing, that statement has had on you.

3. We concluded this chapter by saying, "God plans to turn each of us into His unexpected leaders—men who will reclaim some small part of this world in such a striking way that *only* He can get the glory." Has that happened yet? If not, how does the story of Gideon give you hope that God will use you?

5

DAVID

THE PRINCIPLE OF CORRECTION

HOW GOD RESCUES MEN WHEN THEY GO ASTRAY

Suppose your son knows he shouldn't hit his sister, but he hits her anyway. Then, when you confront him about what he's done, he says, "I'm sorry." You will forgive him, right? Of course. But is that the end of it? Of course not.

Because you love him, you will also want to tutor his heart so that he doesn't repeat the misbehavior. Depending on what you think your son needs, you will correct and restore him with enough severity so that it's not likely to happen again.

As men, our offenses are more complex and the stakes are higher, but our Father's objective is the same. It's to do whatever it takes to correct and restore us to a life of obedience when we go astray.

What we're about to see is that God's discipline is a good thing—

even when it's severe—because that's how He "forces" us back to Him. Yes, God really does use correction to force us back to Himself. The principle for this chapter is,

> God makes men by doing whatever it takes
> to correct and restore us when we go astray.

Nowhere is this principle more vividly illustrated than in the life of King David, whom God called "a man after my own heart" (Acts 13:22).

In the life of David we see how much good a man can do as *an image of God,* yet we also see how much bad that same man can do as *a product of the Fall.*

David's stunning defeat of Goliath as a teenager thrust him into the public spotlight. He became a national hero, a great general, and eventually the king of Israel. God gave him spectacular success in everything because he had a good heart. Unfortunately, that success went to his head and got the better of him. Here's how it happened.

From Hero to Zero

The Bible says, "In the spring, at the time when kings go off to war, *David sent Joab.... But David remained in Jerusalem*" (2 Samuel 11:1). Here's a great problem: If you are where you shouldn't be, you will be tempted to do what you shouldn't do.

One evening David was walking around on the roof of his palace—a place where he shouldn't have been. He should have been leading his army in battle. In the golden hues of dusk, he saw a beautiful woman bathing and, instead of turning away, let his eyes linger.

Can a man look at a beautiful woman and not lust? The answer is yes—but not for very long!

Unfortunately for David, he had too much time on his hands. Overcome by this woman's beauty, he had her brought to him, they slept together, and she became pregnant.

Bathsheba was the wife of Uriah, one of David's mighty men who had gone to war with Joab. Today that would be equivalent to a boss sending a senior employee on a long business trip and then seducing his wife in his absence and getting her pregnant. Sure, it takes two to commit adultery, but aren't we men supposed to be leaders?

To cover his tracks, David arranged to have Bathsheba's husband, Uriah, killed during a fierce battle. After Bathsheba completed the mourning period for her husband, David took her as his wife.

Uncovering the Cover-Up

But God was not happy about what He'd seen David do. There are no "secret sins." Hebrews 4:13 says, "Nothing in all creation is hidden from God's sight. Everything is uncovered and laid bare before the eyes of him to whom we must give account." Proverbs 5:21 tells us, "A man's ways are in full view of the LORD."

Just when David thought the whole situation had blown over and he'd gotten away with it, God sent the prophet Nathan to confront him. Nathan told a parable that made David burn with anger against a rich man who stole from a poor man. Although this next passage is lengthy, be sure to read it through carefully to take in the gravity of it all.

> Then Nathan said to David, "You are [the rich man who abused his power]! This is what the LORD, the God of Israel, says: 'I anointed you king over Israel, and I delivered you from the hand of Saul. I gave your master's house to you, and your master's wives into your arms. I gave you the house of Israel and Judah. And if all this had been too little, I would have given you even more. Why did you despise the word of the LORD by doing what is evil in his eyes? You struck down Uriah the Hittite with the sword and took his wife to be your own. You killed him with the sword of the Ammonites. Now, therefore, the sword will never depart from your house, because you despised me and took the wife of Uriah the Hittite to be your own.'
>
> "This is what the LORD says: 'Out of your own household I am going to bring calamity upon you. Before your very eyes I will take your wives and give them to one who is close to you, and he will lie with your wives in broad daylight. You did it in secret, but I will do this thing in broad daylight before all Israel.'" (2 Samuel 12:7–12)

Do you think God was angry? Look more closely at what the Holy Spirit said through Nathan.

- "Everything you have—respect, honor, power, prosperity—I gave you."
- "If you wanted more, I would have given it to you."
- "Why did you despise the word of the Lord by doing evil?"

- "As a result, the sword will never depart from your house."
- "Your wives will be given to another man who will disgrace them and you."

There's no way around it: God was livid.

Angrily confronted with his sin, David repented:

David said to Nathan, "I have sinned against the LORD."

Nathan replied, "The LORD has taken away your sin. You are not going to die. But because by doing this you have made the enemies of the LORD show utter contempt, the son born to you will die." (verses 13–14)

There's a lot happening in the Nathan verses, but the main principle is that God orchestrated an intervention to confront, rescue, and restore David. David responded in repentance, and his sins were forgiven.

Forgiveness doesn't mean, however, that there won't be consequences.

A MOMENT OF PLEASURE, BUT AT WHAT PRICE?

David paid a huge price for his moment of sexual pleasure and the murderous cover-up that followed. As Nathan predicted:

- His son conceived in adultery did die.
- Another son, Amnon, raped David's daughter Tamar.
- His son Absalom murdered Amnon.
- Later Absalom conspired to overthrow David. He pitched a tent on the roof of his father's palace and slept with his father's concubines.

- Absalom was killed by David's general.
- His son Adonijah led a second conspiracy to take the crown away from David.
- His son Solomon had Adonijah killed for treachery.

Four sons died, two sons conspired against him, and his precious daughter was raped. The tragedies and heartaches suffered by David's family are not unlike those of our Kennedys.

David really was a man after God's own heart. Yet one lusty decision set off a chain reaction that tainted a lifetime of good. Here's how the Bible summarizes his life:

> David had done what was right in the eyes of the LORD and had
> not failed to keep any of the LORD's commands all the days of his
> life—except in the case of Uriah the Hittite. (1 Kings 15:5)

He will always have an asterisk after his name indicating the blot on his character.

Why did God preserve not only a written record of all the good David did but also this exposé of his terrible sin and its fallout? He did it for us.

DESPITE YOUR ASTERISK,
YOU CAN BE FORGIVEN

God wants us to see that if He would forgive David even after adultery and murder, then no one is outside the circle of His mercy and forgiveness. Let's be honest. We all have asterisks by our names for something. Through this story, God wants you to know that, no matter what you've done, it doesn't have to be the end of you. You are never beyond the reach of His gospel. The Holy Spirit speaking through the prophet Isaiah said it best:

> We all, like sheep, have gone astray,
>   each of us has turned to his own way;
> and the LORD has laid on him
>   the iniquity of us all. (Isaiah 53:6)

The penalty for all our sins—past, present, and future—has already been laid on Christ and paid in full. The gospel of Jesus means that no matter what you've done, you can be forgiven.

You may think that because you have failed to manage your household well, have caused your children to wander from the faith, battle an ongoing struggle to love your wife like Christ, have made success an idol, or have committed some truly terrible sin, you've disqualified yourself from grace and are beyond God's reach. That's simply not true. No matter what you've done, you can be forgiven if you will repent of your sins.

YOU CAN NEVER FALL SO FAR THAT GOD CAN'T REACH YOU

God has an altogether different way of thinking about those inevitable times when we, like sheep, go astray. The idea is simple: God will do whatever it takes to get you back. No one who has believed in Christ can ever fall so far that the hand of God will not rescue and restore him. Jesus put it this way:

All that the Father gives me will come to me, and whoever
comes to me I will never drive away.... And this is the will of
him who sent me, that I shall lose none of all that he has given
me, but raise them up at the last day. (John 6:37, 39)

Theologians call this concept "the perseverance of the saints." Or
sometimes "eternal security." It's the doctrine some of us refer to as
"once saved, always saved." The Westminster Confession of Faith explains the details of perseverance like this:

1. "They whom God hath accepted in his Beloved, effectually
   called and sanctified by his Spirit, can neither totally nor
   finally fall away from the state of grace; but shall certainly
   persevere therein to the end, and be eternally saved."

2. "This perseverance of the saints depends, not upon their
   own free-will, but upon the immutability of the decree
   of election, flowing from the free and unchangeable love
   of God the Father; upon the efficacy of the merit and
   intercession of Jesus Christ; the abiding of the Spirit
   and of the seed of God within them; and the nature of
   the covenant of grace; from all which ariseth also the
   certainty and infallibility thereof."

That doesn't mean we're immune from falling into sin. Nor does
it mean we'll get a pass on paying a David-like penalty for those sins.
The confession goes on:

3. "Nevertheless they may, through the temptations of Satan
   and of the world, the prevalency of corruption remaining in
   them, and the neglect of the means of their preservation, fall
   into grievous sins; and for a time continue therein: whereby

they incur God's displeasure, and grieve his Holy Spirit; come to be deprived of some measure of their graces and comforts; have their hearts hardened, and their consciences wounded; hurt and scandalize others; and bring temporal judgments upon themselves."[1]

For example, Lucas received Jesus in high school, but he never grew in his new faith and his heart became hard. If he wasn't working, he was on the golf course, which meant he neglected his wife and children. It was a small, shallow life. He became increasingly miserable and made it a point to make life equally miserable for his wife and especially his oldest son. One day he woke up and it was fifteen years later. He realized his wife couldn't stand him and his son was convinced his dad didn't like him.

Lucas said, "I realized there was something wrong with my family. I realized it was me." But God loved Lucas too much to let him destroy himself. God brought Lucas to his senses (in Bible Time), and he came back to his first love, Jesus. Why did he come back? Certainly not because of anything he initiated. Instead, God made his life so miserable that he had nowhere else to turn.

That's how Lucas got an asterisk next to his name.

It's the same for you. Because He loves you so much, He will not let you destroy yourself. But that doesn't mean you won't have to suffer the consequences.

FORGIVENESS AND CONSEQUENCES TODAY

When I first went into real estate development, I vowed to never personally guarantee a business deal. I would borrow on properties only if

the lender agreed to let the property be the sole collateral for the debt.
I understood this to be a biblical principle.

> Do not be a man who strikes hands in pledge
>   or puts up security for debts;
> if you lack the means to pay,
>   your very bed will be snatched from under you.
>   (Proverbs 22:26–27)

As a result, a lot of really good deals slipped through my fingers.
And then one day I was offered a real estate deal that was almost too
good to be true. But the deal would work only if I would personally
guarantee the debt, which meant that in addition to putting up the
building as collateral I would also have to pledge every other asset I
owned to guarantee repayment of the debt.

After praying about it, I didn't feel comfortable about going forward. But as I said, the deal was almost too good to be true—it was
incredibly tempting. So, like a sheep that *wanted* to be led astray, I
pledged everything I owned to repay the mortgage.

And do you know what? I got away with it—that time. Yet with
one stupid decision, I started down the slippery slope of personally
guaranteeing other real estate and business loans on a regular basis.
Over the next seven years, I amassed an unconscionable amount of
business debt, all of it personally guaranteed. And I never once asked
my wife what she thought about it.

I went on a debt bender for seven years. To be honest, in the bull
market we were in, debt was fun. Leverage let me pretend to have a
bigger business than I really owned.

Then the real estate market collapsed, and in six short months real estate values plummeted 50 percent. The problem was that I had borrowed 75 percent of the higher values. All of my properties were underwater financially—way under. It was fun while it lasted, but the hangover was brutal. I was facing insolvency.

I remember going home for lunch one day. No one was there. As I leaned against the kitchen sink and looked through the window into the sunny backyard, I said out loud, "I am so weary. I just don't know how I can go on for one more day."

But the spiritual toll was even greater. God decided to humble me because I wasn't strong enough to humble myself. When a man gets too big for his britches, the solution is not bigger britches. I was confronted with my sins. It was like Nathan had come back from the grave. Like David, I repented, but there were consequences.

God severely disciplined me for my pride, for making success into an idol, for trying to reinvent God in my imagination as a deity I could control and manipulate to get what I wanted, and for disobeying His Word.

Every day for the next seven years, I woke up fighting to stay solvent. It took seven years to amass an enormous debt. And in a kind of poetic, moral symmetry, it eventually took another seven years to get out of it.

By God's grace and with lots of hard work, I did remain solvent. But those seven years were about the most painful thing I've ever experienced. When we stray, we pay.

Because He loves me so much, God wouldn't let me destroy myself. If it had been up to me, I'm pretty sure I would have continued to cover up my sins and soldier on. Instead, He sovereignly orchestrated an intervention to rescue, correct, and restore. In a word, God "forced" me back into a right relationship with Him.

Now I, too, will always have an asterisk after my name.

It Is Good to Be Afflicted

Terrence, a friend of mine from our Bible study, had a business partner who committed fraud. The state prosecutor assumed Terrence was guilty by association and went after him with a vengeance. Many of us prayed for and encouraged him during a drawn-out, four-year pretrial roller coaster.

The battle to clear his name eventually cleaned Terrence out financially. The stress became too much. In the end he pleaded "no contest," accepting five years of probation rather than face a lengthy court fight he couldn't afford. Now Terrence has an asterisk by his name too.

It was a tough price to pay. But it was also necessary. The firestorm made him sensitive to the fact that he had been cutting too many corners. Although he wasn't guilty of the crime he was accused of, he was guilty of other sins, such as pride, greed, and idolatry. He had taken charge of his own life. He wasn't living an obedient, holy, Christ-centered life. Once the legal uncertainty was behind him, Terrence told me something I'll never forget. He said, "It was what I needed. I needed to be broken."

That's the same conclusion David came to. By the time his nightmare was over, David realized how good it was that God loved him enough to spank him. He, or someone just like him, said,

- "Before I was afflicted I went astray, but now I obey your word" (Psalm 119:67).

- "It was good for me to be afflicted so that I might learn your decrees" (verse 71).
- "In faithfulness you have afflicted me" (verse 75).

David learned obedience by being disciplined. Obedience to Christ is the trademark of a biblical Christian. If we will not obey His Word, then God will graciously discipline us until we do. His discipline forces us to seek the God that success makes us think we don't need.

> Our earthly fathers disciplined us for a few years, doing the best they knew how. But God's discipline is always good for us, so that we might share in his holiness. No discipline is enjoyable while it is happening—it's painful! But afterward there will be a peaceful harvest of right living for those who are trained in this way. (Hebrews 12:10–11, NLT)

The inexplicable peace and joy that follow God's loving discipline so far exceed the pinnacle moments of a secular life that it is impossible to explain to anyone who hasn't experienced it for himself. Thank God that He gives us what we need, not what we want!

If you have gone astray, or when you do, what can you expect God to do?

STEPS TO RESTORATION

God has a process of correction and restoration that starts the moment we go astray. The Bible says the Holy Spirit is grieved when we sin (see Ephesians 4:30). The work of restoration is the work of the Holy

Spirit. He is the one who convicts us of our sin—which is the first step to restoration. Jesus said,

> It is for your good that I am going away. Unless I go away, the
> Counselor [the Holy Spirit] will not come to you; but if I go, I
> will send him to you. When he comes, he will convict the world
> of guilt in regard to sin and righteousness and judgment: in
> regard to sin, because men do not believe in me. (John 16:7–9)

Because of Bible Time, the conviction of sin can happen quickly or it can take a long time. For David, we know God sent Nathan before the birth of the son who died, so less than nine months had passed from the adultery. In the case of Lucas, it took fifteen years. I held out for a dozen years, but Terrence saw the error of his ways in less than four years.

God may send a friend who speaks into your life. Or He may orchestrate your circumstances so that you are miserable. You may hear directly from the Holy Spirit. However God sets the principle of correction into motion, it will always include His Word—even if it's just a few words repeated by a stranger.

> The word of God is living and active. Sharper than any double-
> edged sword, it penetrates even to dividing soul and spirit,
> joints and marrow; it judges the thoughts and attitudes of the
> heart. (Hebrews 4:12)

The second step to restoration is repentance. Seeds of regret are sown in our hearts. Once our hearts have been truly pierced by godly sorrow, we cry out to God for forgiveness. Second Corinthians 7:8–10 describes how it works:

> Even if I caused you sorrow by my letter, I do not regret it. Though I did regret it—I see that my letter hurt you, but only for a little while—yet now I am happy, not because you were made sorry, but because your sorrow led you to repentance. For you became sorrowful as God intended and so were not harmed in any way by us. Godly sorrow brings repentance that leads to salvation and leaves no regret, but worldly sorrow brings death.

Are you there? If so, you can repent with any words you want. If you're looking for some guidance, you can use the prayer of repentance David offered in response to Nathan, found in Psalm 51. Here are a few of the key verses:

> Have mercy on me, O God,
>   according to your unfailing love;
> according to your great compassion
>   blot out my transgressions.
> Wash away all my iniquity
>   and cleanse me from my sin.
>
> For I know my transgressions,
>   and my sin is always before me....
>
> Create in me a pure heart, O God,
>   and renew a steadfast spirit within me.

Do not cast me from your presence
    or take your Holy Spirit from me.…

You do not delight in sacrifice, or I would bring it;
    you do not take pleasure in burnt offerings.
The sacrifices of God are a broken spirit;
    a broken and contrite heart,
    O God, you will not despise. (verses 1–3, 10–11, 16–17)

If you have prayed with godly sorrow, then you are forgiven. Nothing else is required.

However, the third step toward restoration is consequences. Sometimes the marriage cannot be reconciled after an affair. Sometimes the debts can't be paid off and you have to go through bankruptcy. Sometimes your uncontrollable temper will cost you your job. Sometimes your pride will taint your reputation. And if you have taken something that doesn't belong to you, you should make restitution as soon as possible.

The final step in restoration is to guard your heart as you go forward. Whenever I talk about David, men resonate deeply with the idea of being "a man after God's own heart." They want what David had. And if they already have their asterisk, they want it even more.

Proverbs 4:23 says, "Above all else, guard your heart, for it is the wellspring of life." How can we guard our hearts "above all else"? The best way to guard your heart is to become a man of the Word—read it, memorize it, quote it, live it. The Word of God has unique spiritual power not only to rebuke and correct us but also to teach and train us. Paul put it to Timothy like this:

From infancy you have known the holy Scriptures, which are
able to make you wise for salvation through faith in Christ
Jesus. All Scripture is God-breathed and is useful for teaching,
rebuking, correcting and training in righteousness, so that the
man of God may be thoroughly equipped for every good work.
(2 Timothy 3:15–17)

Another way to guard your heart is to be the same man in private
that you are in public. It's the idea of living "one life, one way."

Once I scheduled one of our IT men to work on my computer,
even though I knew I needed to leave for a few hours while he was
there.

I don't know about your computer, but mine is the history of me.
All of my correspondence is on there, all of my Internet history, all of
my writing, all of my private journals, my most inner thoughts, everything I have ever written just for my own eyes, the letters I've written
and not sent when I was just trying to get something off my chest—it's
all on there.

Because I've been practicing "one life, one way" for decades, I was
able to walk away from my computer with zero concern about what
that man might find. Now, hopefully he has enough integrity not to
go snooping around in my private files, but if he did, it's okay, because
I have nothing to hide.

One reason I am so careful to guard my heart is that I've cultivated
an extreme sense of the immediate presence of Christ. I'm not saying
I don't sin—I sin every day. But when I'm in a room by myself, I don't
really think about being in a room by myself. I think of being in a
room with Jesus.

But we cannot guard our hearts alone. I can't help but wonder how David's life might have turned out differently if he had been part of a small group of men who were doing life together, praying for each other, and holding each other accountable. Why didn't Joab call David out on his dumb decision? It's dangerous not to have a friend who will say, "Are you crazy? You can't do that." That's why we need some brothers to keep us from going astray.

But when we do go astray, isn't it good to know that God will do whatever it takes to correct and restore us to a life of obedience?

For Reflection and Discussion

1. How has God corrected and restored you from a sin that would have destroyed you?

2. Why did David say it was good for him to be afflicted in Psalm 119:67, 71, and 75?

3. Of course, it would be better not to sin. But God has given us David as an example of the lengths to which He will go to correct and restore us to obedience when we do sin. What have you learned or been reminded of that you really needed to hear?

6

SOLOMON

THE PRINCIPLE OF SUCCESS THAT MATTERS

How God Shows Men the True Path to Happiness

One day when I was a young businessman, I came home driving a recently acquired luxury car to a lovely home and a beautiful wife. If you had seen me that day, you would have thought, *That guy has everything going his way.*

I pulled into the garage, put the door down, and began to kick the wall with the bottom of my foot. I kicked until I could kick no more. I was just so frustrated. How could I have everything I had ever wanted and be so miserable?

I had been so sure that money would solve my problems and that success would make me happy. I was meeting all my goals. (At the time I thought it was because I was so smart. In hindsight I realize it was because of a good economy.) But the more I achieved, the deeper I sank into despair. Sometimes I think the poor have at least one advantage over the affluent—they can still cling to the illusion that money will make them happy! But I had found a type of success that didn't really matter. It was empty.

As someone who works with men as my vocation, I find surprisingly few men—Christian or otherwise—who are genuinely content with who they are and what they do. I have several theories, but they all point back to a man's thinking he can have the best of both worlds—the best of a Christian worldview and the best of what the world has to offer. This error is so much more prevalent than you may first think and, as you will see, is nothing new.

How about you? In spite of all your blessings, do you also have a sense that something is missing? Do you also find meaning elusive? If so, I've got some good news for you. Things are about to change. It's going to get so much better. That's because God's plan is to use that sense of frustration as a tool to chisel you into the man He wants you to be. You're about to learn the principle of a success that really matters:

> God makes men by making it impossible
> for us to find lasting happiness in any
> pursuit apart from Him.

Of course, down through history men and women have missed God's cue—badly and repeatedly, often for decades—before He finally gets their attention. The plot line looks something like this: they pursue happiness according to their own best wisdom, they don't attain happiness, they kick the wall until they can kick no more—but then they don't change course. They just keep doing what didn't work, hoping for different results. And they settle for less, trying to dull their disappointment and frustration with substances or activities that help numb the pain.

What a waste! Thankfully, the Bible offers the ideal mentor for understanding how this principle works: King Solomon, a son of David and Bathsheba. As far as we can tell, Solomon never stopped trying to do it his way…but at least he took excellent notes.

You know Solomon. He's the guy who accumulated more wisdom, wealth, and fame than perhaps any man in history. Today the leaders of NATO, the United Nations, and the G8 nations would all come to seek his counsel. He was richer than Carlos Slim, Warren Buffett, and Bill Gates put together. No man was ever more blessed by God than Solomon.

But then he lost his way.

Solomon pursued every possible avenue to find meaning apart from God. He ended up hating his life.

God doesn't want that to happen to you. In this chapter we'll look at Solomon's experiences for insights into how God wants to lead us into holiness and make us more like Jesus.

A Man with Unlimited Potential

Early in his kingly career, Solomon had a rare experience with God. He'd gone on a spiritual pilgrimage to Gibeon, where the Lord appeared to him during the night in a dream. God said to him, "Ask for whatever you want me to give you" (1 Kings 3:5).

Solomon humbled himself and said to the Lord, "Give your servant a discerning heart to govern your people and to distinguish between right and wrong. For who is able to govern this great people of yours?" (verse 9). The Lord was pleased with his response and said to Solomon,

> Since you have asked for this and not for long life or wealth for yourself, nor have asked for the death of your enemies but for discernment in administering justice, I will do what you have asked. I will give you a wise and discerning heart, so that there will never have been anyone like you, nor will there ever be. Moreover, I will give you what you have not asked for—both riches and honor—so that in your lifetime you will have no equal among kings. And if you walk in my ways and obey my statutes and commands as David your father did, I will give you a long life. (verses 11–14)

And that's exactly what happened. Along with knowing how to dispense justice in his kingdom, Solomon acquired unparalleled amounts of money, power, and fame. He built the temple of God for which his father, David, had assembled the materials. The architectural design was stupendous. That great edifice would be worth billions of dollars today. There was no building like it in the whole world.

But that was just the beginning of what Solomon would accomplish. He was curious, tireless, multitalented. In fact, Solomon was the original Renaissance man. He wrote the books of Proverbs, Ecclesiastes, and Song of Songs. His poems, proverbs, and prose still rate among the greatest literary achievements of all time. He was the Pulitzer Prize winner and the poet laureate of his day.

He also loved to study plant and animal life—he was a botanist and zoologist. He was a shipping magnate who built a vast fleet of merchant ships. He was a collector of beautiful Egyptian horses. He was the leading patron of the arts for his kingdom. There seemed to be hardly any area of human endeavor that didn't interest him.

He was a teacher too. People came from nations near and far so they could learn and gain from his wisdom. When the queen of Sheba saw that he could answer any of her questions, and when she saw the splendor and majesty of his kingdom, she said, "I had heard about you, but I couldn't believe it until I saw it with my own eyes. Now that I've seen it, I realize they didn't even tell me half of the story, so vast is your wisdom and wealth!" (see 1 Kings 10:6–7).

Solomon was the greatest man of his era. But along the way, something went terribly wrong. He lost his desire to put God first. He began, instead, to look to his own accomplishments, power, wealth, and pleasures for meaning.

And it wasn't working.

THE SORROWS OF SOLOMON

Solomon began the book of Ecclesiastes by writing,

"Meaningless! Meaningless!"
    says the Teacher.
"Utterly meaningless!
    Everything is meaningless." (Ecclesiastes 1:2)

Even though God had blessed him with everything a man could ever want, he wasn't happy. Despite all that money, all that power, and all that wisdom, Solomon struggled for decades to find a sense of meaning and purpose. He always carried around the feeling that his life was futile. He was riddled with angst.

Most of us know how he felt, don't we? Though we may not live our lives on a scale remotely matching Solomon's, we've been where he was, spiritually and emotionally speaking. And so we each owe a debt to Solomon, because he dedicated his life to solving this problem of life's apparent meaninglessness. He wanted to know how a man could have everything he wanted and still not be happy. He said, "I wanted to see what was worthwhile for men to do under heaven during the few days of their lives" (Ecclesiastes 2:3).

What was his strategy? Solomon decided that he would explore every possible earthly avenue to find meaning apart from God. "I devoted myself to study and to explore by wisdom all that is done under heaven," he reported (Ecclesiastes 1:13). He tried wisdom, knowledge, the arts, literature, science, commerce, horticulture, exploration, folly, wine, wealth, sex, power, prestige, great projects, building a reputation, and throwing himself into his work. Yet nothing satisfied him.

Here are a few of Solomon's exploits in his own words:

> I undertook great projects: I built houses for myself and planted vineyards. I made gardens and parks and planted all kinds of fruit trees in them. I made reservoirs to water groves of flourishing trees. I bought male and female slaves and had other slaves who were born in my house. I also owned more herds and flocks than anyone in Jerusalem before me. I amassed silver and gold for myself, and the treasure of kings and provinces.

I acquired men and women singers, and a harem as well—the
delights of the heart of man. I became greater by far than anyone
in Jerusalem before me. In all this my wisdom stayed with me.

I denied myself nothing my eyes desired;
    I refused my heart no pleasure.
My heart took delight in all my work,
    and this was the reward for all my labor.
Yet when I surveyed all that my hands had done
    and what I had toiled to achieve,
everything was meaningless, a chasing after the wind;
    nothing was gained under the sun. (Ecclesiastes 2:4–11)

And what did he conclude from all this? "I hated life," he said,
"because the work that is done under the sun was grievous to me. All
of it is meaningless, a chasing after the wind" (verse 17).

Solomon no doubt assumed he would find what he was looking
for in these earthly avenues of success. But he did not.

I've been there. You've been there too. Solomon's story is our story.
God put this story in the Bible to teach us how to find—and not
find—meaning.

Solomon's mistake was to pursue meaning apart from God. The
message for us is clear. Apart from God, life has no meaning. Apart
from God, life has no enduring happiness. Apart from God, we get
only the shadow of the thing we want. Solomon chased the shadow;
he didn't chase the real thing.

That's why I say we all owe Solomon a debt of gratitude. He found and teased out every possible way in the world to *not* find meaning. And God, in His grace, preserved this grand story so that you and I could be spared the sorrows of Solomon.

The Research Results

The book of Ecclesiastes reads like a case study for a PhD dissertation. It has all the elements: the purpose of the study, the problem, the research question, findings, conclusions, a summary, and recommendations. Let's look at one of Solomon's main findings and conclusions:

> [God] has made everything beautiful in its time. He has also set eternity in the hearts of men; yet they cannot fathom what God has done from beginning to end. I know that there is nothing better for men than to be happy and do good while they live. That everyone may eat and drink, and find satisfaction in all his toil—this is the gift of God. I know that everything God does will endure forever; nothing can be added to it and nothing taken from it. *God does it so that men will revere him.* (Ecclesiastes 3:11–14)

And there it is. God will not force you to revere Him, but He will make it impossible for you to be happy unless you do. God made it impossible for you to find meaning in any earthly pursuit apart from Him, because if you could, you would. And then you wouldn't revere Him.

Solomon has demolished the possibility of anybody ever credibly arguing that you can find meaning in life apart from God. It cannot be done. And yet half of us will put down this book and spend the rest of the day chasing an idol we think will make us happy.

Maybe it's a level of career success that is your idol. You might think, *If I could just pull this big deal off, that would do it for me.* Or you might think, *If I could just get that beautiful woman to love me, I would be happy forever.* Or, *If I could live on the beach that I see on my computer background...or write that novel...or get my master's degree...or retire early...or get the lead in the play...or buy a new sports car...or...or...* Whatever worldly pursuit you're putting your hope in to give your life meaning and happiness, Solomon has already proved that it won't.

And besides, it's not really the beach scene on a computer background that we want. What we really want is the idea of how we think that beach (or big deal or woman or achievement) would make us feel. That's the deception of an idol. Let's face it. If you were actually at that beach, you'd be hot, sticky, sandy, covered with mosquito bites, sunburned, and longing for Internet service.

So how did Solomon get off track? And what can we learn from him to help us not make those same mistakes?

HOW WE GET OFF TRACK

After 1 Kings 1–10 recounts Solomon's brilliant career, chapter 11 starts out with these telling words: "King Solomon, however..." You know it is not going to be good when there is a "however." And guess what? It's not.

King Solomon, however, loved many foreign women.... They were from nations about which the LORD had told the Israelites,

"You must not intermarry with them, because they will surely
turn your hearts after their gods." Nevertheless, Solomon held
fast to them in love. (1 Kings 11:1–2)

Solomon loved the ladies. He married a bunch of them. Actually,
he had seven hundred wives and three hundred mistresses! Today we'd
call him a sex addict. He chose the carnal pleasures of this world over
the commands of God. The results were devastating.

As Solomon grew old, his wives turned his heart after other
gods, and his heart was not fully devoted to the LORD his God,
as the heart of David his father had been. He followed Ashto-
reth the goddess of the Sidonians, and Molech the detestable
god of the Ammonites. So Solomon did evil in the eyes of the
LORD; he did not follow the LORD completely, as David his
father had done. (verses 4–6)

I find it absolutely fascinating that the two issues that led to Solomon's downfall are as prevalent and relevant today as they were back
then. These are by no means the only ways men get off track today, but
they are very common. Let's take each of these two in turn and see why
it's impossible for them to make a man happy.

Sex

You may be thinking, *Solomon was this rich guy who had sex with a
thousand women. How is that relevant to me?*

Actually, his story is very relevant because of what Jesus said about
adultery. Do you remember? He said if you even look at a woman

lustfully you have already committed adultery with her in your heart (see Matthew 5:28). But how many of us have looked lustfully at a thousand women?

Let's do the math. Have you lusted once a month, once a week, or once a day? How about twice a day? Or several times a day? If you lusted just once a day for three years, that will get you to one thousand women—neck and neck with Solomon.

So let's keep it real. Don't think it could never happen to you, because it already has. When it comes to sexual immorality, we are no different from Solomon in the eyes of Jesus.

One morning at our Bible study I decided to teach on 1 Corinthians 6:18, which says, "Flee from sexual immorality." As I pulled out of my garage and started driving through my neighborhood to teach it, I saw a woman walking her dog. She was wearing short shorts and a tank top. I thought she was very beautiful, and admiring beauty is normal…but not if it leads to lust. Then I thought, *It's a good thing I'm in the car. I can flee!*

Thankfully, it was only a temptation. But that's the point—temptations are so *tempting*.

Why flee from sexual immorality? All other sins are outside our bodies, but sexual sin is against our own bodies. "Do you not know that your body is a temple of the Holy Spirit, who is in you, whom you have received from God? You are not your own; you were bought at a price. Therefore honor God with your body" (verses 19–20).

But Solomon didn't flee.

Too often we don't flee either.

Sexual immorality—or any of the many other sins that we can easily fall into, such as pride, cheating on taxes, gossip, or wanting to "be a somebody"—takes our affections away from God and puts them onto selfish, sinful pursuits. We *think* we're headed toward happiness, and in fact we might temporarily get to enjoy pleasures—Solomon did. But it will never last. It will always end in futility and frustration. That's God's order of things.

But that's only part of the problem.

Wanting the Best of Both Worlds

Solomon's sex addiction wasn't the only thing that kept him from lasting happiness. The deeper problem was that "his wives turned his heart after other gods" (1 Kings 11:4).

The reason God didn't want Solomon—or us—to marry non-believers is the problem of being unequally yoked. What man doesn't want to please his wife and make her happy? But Solomon took wives who worshiped other gods. And instead of having them go to his temple, he started going to theirs.

Solomon tried to have his cake and eat it too. He tried to keep everyone happy by blending faith in the one true God with the different belief systems of the pagan nations with which he had intermarried. Short version of the results? His wives turned his heart away from God and toward idols.

There is a technical word for this: *syncretism*. It means blending different religious or belief systems together. And this, of course, dilutes and distorts the truth of God. That is exactly what happened in Solomon's life. And that's exactly what happened to me too.

Once I realized that money wouldn't solve my problems and that success wouldn't make me happy, I became a Christian. But in many ways I only added Jesus to my life without subtracting my materialism.

Like Solomon, I wanted the best of both worlds—the peace of God and the spoils of worldly ambition.

In business we have an axiom that states, "Your system is perfectly designed to produce the results you are getting." It works for our belief systems too. In other words, we each have a belief system that is perfectly designed to produce the results we are getting.

Solomon got off track because he had a systems problem. He had a belief system that was perfectly designed to produce a sense of meaninglessness. Somewhere along the line, he stopped putting God first over everything else. He didn't "seek first his kingdom and his righteousness" (Matthew 6:33). His "other gods" became a temptation and a trap. He pursued a success that *didn't* matter because it *couldn't* matter.

That's because God has a system too. A system perfectly designed to produce an abundant life. But in God's system, no one can have the best of both worlds. Jesus put it like this:

No one can serve two masters. Either he will hate the one and love the other, or he will be devoted to the one and despise the other. You cannot serve both God and Money. (Matthew 6:24)

That's the kind of strict limitation God's system has put on all earthly pursuits apart from Him. So beware of syncretism. Don't try to have your cake and eat it too. Don't try to have the best of both worlds. If you are a follower of Jesus, do not intermarry your faith in Him with competing, nonbiblical beliefs that are current in the culture, such as same-sex marriage. You cannot get where you want to go, and where

God wants you to be, if your heart is divided between Christ and any other gods.

Are you beginning to see how our best efforts to find meaning and happiness can actually take us away from the only path that can deliver those outcomes?

If you would say, "Yep, Pat, I *do* see, and I think I've gotten as lost as Solomon," be encouraged. God's path is still true. He created you for a purpose, with fulfillment and plenty of happiness along the way. And He is ready to reconstruct your life.

THE CONCLUSION OF THE MATTER

A Christian friend of mine has had trouble making peace with the fact that worldly success has eluded him his entire life. He called recently to say that for six months he has been on a potent antidepressant to counteract the deep sadness he was feeling.

Here's what's ironic. He is as depressed that he didn't achieve worldly success as I was depressed when I did. Two opposite circumstantial results; same depressive outcome. How does that happen?

Don't get me wrong. There is no sin in worldly success—whether it's business success or something else—per se. But because worldly success is such a seductive idol, God in His wisdom has made it impossible for worldly success alone to satisfy.

When we make anything into an idol, God will deal with us in one of three ways:

- He will withhold the thing we think we can't live without.
- He will remove the thing we think we can't live without.
- Or He will give us so much of it that we gag on it.

I've experienced all three, and possibly you have too.

Here's the core human problem. If you or I could find satisfaction in any worldly success apart from God, we would. So to protect us from our own sinful natures, God in His grace frustrates our ambitions when they would destroy us. And it's not really worldly success we want anyway, but rather we want the security, contentment, peace, and joy we think it will give us. By giving—or not giving—us worldly success, our jealous God is teaching us to be satisfied in Him alone. We should enjoy nice things if and when we can, but He is our security, contentment, peace, and joy.

Are you off track? Or headed that way?

Under the inspiration of the Holy Spirit, Solomon wrote Ecclesiastes so we would see what happened to him, how he blew it, and how we can be equipped to not make the same mistakes.

I think it's highly probable that God put the example of Solomon's matchless wealth, power, and wisdom in His Word so none of us can ever say, "If I just had enough money, power, and wisdom, then I would be happy."

After a life devoted to discovering what is worthwhile for men to do, and after finding that apart from God life has no meaning, Solomon concluded Ecclesiastes with this sobering advice:

> Here is the conclusion of the matter:
> Fear God and keep his commandments,
>   for this is the whole duty of man.
> For God will bring every deed into judgment,
>   including every hidden thing,
>   whether it is good or evil. (12:13–14)

Fear (or revere) God and keep His commandments.[1] Most of us already know this truth. The most difficult lessons to learn, however, are usually the ones we already know.

It is impossible for you and me to find happiness—real happiness, lasting happiness—in any pursuit apart from God. That's what Solomon figured out the hard way so that we wouldn't have to.

For Reflection and Discussion

1. What was Solomon's quest, and how did he get off track?
2. The principle for this chapter is that *God makes men by making it impossible for us to find lasting happiness in any pursuit apart from Him.* Where have you been looking for happiness apart from God? Where are you trying to have the best of both worlds?
3. What did you find out from Solomon that you needed to know? How can his conclusions keep you on track or get you back on track? Where do you think you will be in ten years if you don't make a course correction? What do you want to do?

7

NEHEMIAH

THE PRINCIPLE OF
A PASSIONATE CALLING

How God Calls Men to Action

W hen I was a young man with raging emotions and no direction, I didn't have a clue what manhood was all about. Then
some men took me under their wings to disciple and mentor me on
what it looks like to be a godly man, husband, and father. Because of
them, my life has turned out so much better than I could have ever
imagined. Those early lessons prepared me for the twists and turns life
would bring my way.

The lessons in Christian manhood that my dad received were very
different. No men came alongside him when he was a young husband
and father. He was left on his own to do the best he could. Without the
guidance of mature Christian men, my dad was ill prepared for what

would be required of him. Even though my dad was a Christian, he experienced a very different outcome from his life than I've been getting from mine. Because my dad was cheated out of the life he wanted—and because I know why he was—God has given me a passionate calling to help men become disciples of our Lord and Savior Jesus.

Men's discipleship is the deeply felt need that really stirs me, grips me, and gets me out of bed. It breaks my heart to see any man not have the opportunity to become the man God wants him to be.

My friend Rod's passion, however, is the homeless. Every Friday morning before coming to our Bible study, Rod goes to the McDonald's down by our bus station and buys coffee for homeless men. He says, "Every week it's different. I never know what's going to happen. But every time I show up, so does God."

And Eric's calling is marriage. Several years ago he had an affair that devastated his marriage and alienated his children. Eric and his wife, both Christians, decided to work through the pain—and was it ever painful. Yet God empowered them to restore their marriage, and today they are stronger than before. Through the tears, God gave both Eric and his wife a deep burden and heartache for other couples having similar problems. Today they teach marriage classes at their church and counsel couples in trouble.

How about you? What is something that is breaking your heart?

Like Rod, Eric, and me, wherever you most personally feel the pain of the lack of God's presence and power is where God will most likely give you a burden to do something about it. Responding to the burden God puts on your heart is how you put yourself into the thick of what God is doing in the world. You can make a huge difference for God. In this chapter you'll learn how God provides to make that happen. The principle is,

> God makes men by turning what breaks
> our hearts into a passionate calling to help
> redeem some broken part of His world.

I can't think of a better example of how God does this than the epic story of Nehemiah. God had an important calling in mind for Nehemiah, a role that would help restore his nation at a point in its history when it could have gone either way.

It's Enough to Make a Grown Man Weep

First, some context. The Jewish nation had been exiled to Babylon for seventy years. The Persians then conquered the Babylonians and allowed the captive Jews to return to Jerusalem if they wanted to. By the time of Nehemiah, a portion of the Jewish people had been back in their homeland for about a century. Ezra had already helped rebuild the temple, but the city and especially its protective walls were still in ruins.

Nehemiah was one of the Jews still living in Babylon, where he held the important job of cupbearer to the king. The cupbearer tasted the king's wine to make sure it wasn't poisoned. This meant he was a trusted member of the king's inner circle.

One day he received a firsthand report from his brother about what was going on back in Jerusalem. "Those who survived the exile and are back in the province are in great trouble and disgrace. The wall of Jerusalem is broken down, and its gates have been burned with fire" (Nehemiah 1:3).

Imagine if a century after the War of 1812 our Capitol and White House were still not rebuilt. Can you picture the weakness that would symbolize and the sense of national disgrace Americans would feel? That's what the Jews were experiencing. That's what Nehemiah experienced personally when he heard the report. It was enough to make a grown man cry. He wrote, "When I heard these things, I sat down and wept. For some days I mourned and fasted and prayed before the God of heaven" (verse 4).

What great need do you see around you that makes you want to weep? That will tell you a lot about the burden God wants to put on your heart. Your next step is to find out what God wants you to do about it.

How to Process the Weight of a Burden

Nehemiah faced what we call a "wicked" problem—a problem that is either highly resistant to solutions or cannot be solved at all. His nation's restoration had stalled. Something was broken. The people were still in bondage. They hadn't done what God expected of them. The national redemption was incomplete. It was heartbreaking news, and Nehemiah took it personally. Listen to his prayer of repentance:

> I confess the sins we Israelites, including myself and my father's
> house, have committed against you. We have acted very wick-

edly toward you. We have not obeyed the commands, decrees and laws you gave your servant Moses. (verses 6–7)

At first, all Nehemiah knew was that he had a heavy heart. But instead of acting in his own strength or wisdom, he humbled himself, prayed, sought God, and repented of their wicked ways—just as it says to do in 2 Chronicles 7:14.

The first step to solve any problem related to sin and disobedience is to pray a prayer of humble repentance. Repentance sets the stage for everything good that follows. Repentance necessarily precedes vision or a plan or a solution.

On the heels of Nehemiah's prayer, God gave him a vision to solve his nation's problem. Whether Nehemiah received his vision immediately or it took time for him to process, we don't know. As far as I can tell, God has no formula for giving men visions. But we do know that four months later the king noticed he was sad. This gave Nehemiah the opening he needed.

> The king said to me, "What is it you want?"
> Then I prayed to the God of heaven, and I answered the king, "If it pleases the king and if your servant has found favor in his sight, let him send me to the city in Judah where my fathers are buried so that I can rebuild it." (Nehemiah 2:4–5)

Don't miss this sequence of how God called Nehemiah to his specific task: first came the heartbreaking weight of a burden, followed by a deep sense of sorrow and repentance, which led to a new vision to do something about the problem.

Only then did he take action.

Lots of problems trouble us, of course, but they don't motivate us enough to take action. However, when you feel so deeply about a problem that you're inspired to get involved, that's a *calling*. When the Holy Spirit gives you a burden that weighs so heavily on you that you feel compelled to do something about it or you will go crazy, you now have a calling on your life.

What problem grabs your heart like that?

YOU ARE THE PLAN

Nehemiah sensed that God had a calling on his life, and he did something about it. He asked for a leave of absence from his job so he could go to Jerusalem and oversee rebuilding the broken-down wall. He also asked the king for the documents he would need to guarantee a safe trip and the materials he would need once he arrived. Nehemiah reported, "Because the gracious hand of my God was upon me, the king granted my requests" (Nehemiah 2:8).

But once Nehemiah was back in Jerusalem, the mission was not easy. He did rebuild the wall, because God was with him. But he also experienced fierce opposition. That's a unique part of how God makes men. He will give you a passionate calling to do something for His glory, but often those who oppose Him don't make it easy. We've seen that in every chapter. Abraham's long wait. Joseph's harsh treatment. The pushback Moses got from his own people. God's favor often is accompanied by trials.

So here's the pattern we learn from Nehemiah. At the point of repentance, God will send a man. God is always on the lookout for a man who will see—really see—some broken part of His creation, feel the sting, carry the burden, lead in repentance, and humbly feel compelled to act as God's agent to redeem what has been broken or lost. He prepares this man for the task and provides whatever is needed for him to carry it out—but rarely without opposition.

That is how God is redeeming culture. That's how God is rescuing the poor. That's how God is overcoming racism. That's how God is countering violence to the unborn. That's how God is restoring marriages. That's how God is saving the lost. That's how God is transforming men who do not know their identity. He does all these things, and more, by selecting specific men (and of course women too) and giving them a burden that ultimately leads them to act.

This is how God does things. God has a plan. It's you. You are the plan. You are God's plan to redeem and change the world.

This idea stirs something deep inside us as men, doesn't it? That's because the need to make a difference is such a deeply embedded part of our nature.

So let me tell you how you can apply Nehemiah's story to your own situation. The question you need to ask is, What makes me weep, mourn, fast, pray, repent, have a vision, and want to act? If you open up yourself to Him with this question, God *will* give you a passionate burden to redeem some broken part of His world—a problem that can be solved only by you releasing the power of God and His gospel.

For Nehemiah, it was the broken-down wall of his homeland. What is it for you? That is where God wants to use you. Or, if you don't already know your burden, how can you identify it? You may find the answer surprising.

Identifying Your Burden

If you want to be involved in redeeming what has been lost, then identify a place where the creation is not working as God intended. It should be a place where the particular need touches your whole heart—intellect, will, and emotions.

Wherever the battle rages for *you* is where God will give you that burden. You may feel it, as Nehemiah did, in an area where you have obvious opportunity and skill. But you should not be surprised, as we learned from Gideon, if you feel your burden in an area of weakness. Wherever your God-given burden leads you is where you are needed. That is where God can use you to make a difference.

For example, if you've struggled with pornography, God may give you a burden for other men who share that struggle. If you have survived a severe marriage crisis, God may give you a burden for other men whose marriages are in trouble. Maybe your burden is for families, broken families, or your own family. Maybe it's for the lost. Maybe your burden is for the poor. Maybe it's the unborn. Maybe you spent decades stuck in a job you hated, and your burden is to help men find work they can love.

Maybe you ache for your church to disciple men—you want to use some of the same skills that work for you in business to lead men to become more like Jesus. Maybe your burden is for young men who are struggling with their identity and turned loose in the world to suffocate under the weight of what they don't know because they've never been mentored. Perhaps the breakdown in society and the public square weighs heavy on your mind. Or maybe you feel the danger of the spiritual decay in our culture.

My computer desktop photo is a satellite picture of Earth. It reminds me of the eternal perspective of a Christian. I see a tiny globe where God is doing things so much greater and bigger than I can even imagine.

Wherever you are in the process of finding and fulfilling your calling, God will give you what you need so that you, along with Nehemiah, can say, "Because the gracious hand of my God was upon me."

So whether you're a relatively new Christian or you have been walking with Christ for decades, ask God to help you see what He sees so you can do what He wants you to do.

FOUR SCENARIOS FOR YOUR PASSIONATE CALLING

Your burden may be as distant as a remote foreign village, but it may also be as near as your immediate family or neighborhood. You could also be at any one of several different stages in responding to that burden. Let's look at four possible scenarios in which you may find yourself.

Scenario 1: "I Don't Know What to Do"

First, perhaps you don't have a burden. What can you do about that?

Sometimes you need a hug, but sometimes you need a kick in the pants. This is the latter. If you don't have a burden, it's because you're not listening. If you don't see a problem that breaks your heart, you're walking around with your eyes shut.

There are so many parts of this world that need to be redeemed either in culture or lost souls. There are so many practical things you can do. Open your eyes, for crying out loud! The broken places are *everywhere*. If you do not have a burden, you're not looking. You're just not seeing what's out there. Could it be that your life is just too comfortable at the moment?

A congressman once told me he had never noticed how many people around him were in so much pain until he experienced a personal crisis himself. "My crisis," he said, "opened my eyes to see what had always been there. But I was too self-absorbed to see it." His pain helped him become the man God wanted him to be. The Bible puts it this way: "We must go through many hardships to enter the kingdom of God" (Acts 14:22).

God is gracious. Now you know. He wants you to see what He sees so that you can do what He wants you to do. He wants you to have that burden. He wants you to feel the sting of the lack of the gospel in some broken corner of His world. I suggest you pray and ask God to let you feel the weight of a burden that makes you want to weep, mourn, fast, pray, repent, and do something about it.

Scenario 2: "I'm Reluctant to Begin"

Let's say God has given you a burden for something important, and you know exactly what it is, but you have not yet acted.

What made Nehemiah different from other men (and probably why God has preserved his story) is that when he felt the burden, Nehemiah did not refuse God. When his burden drove him to his knees, the man did not refuse. When his burden became a calling, the man did not refuse. When his calling became a vision, the man still did not refuse. And when the opportunity to execute the vision presented itself, the man didn't falter. He trusted that God would rebuild the wall that would restore the nation that would redeem the world. And that's exactly what happened.

The game changer was that Nehemiah acted. Here's a second kick in the pants. If you feel the ache of a burden but have not acted, you need to understand that you are being disobedient to God. The apostle Paul said, "I was not disobedient to the vision from heaven" (Acts 26:19). That's where you need to end up too.

And I know this about you: you sincerely want to do something powerful for God and to be God's redemptive agent in the world and to make a difference. That's why you're reading this book, right? So act on your better instincts.

Scenario 3: "I'm Trying, but to Be Honest, It's a Struggle"

You have a burden, you've acted, but now it's turning out to be much harder than you expected. This is a common scenario for would-be Nehemiahs. That's why you need Paul's encouragement: "Let us not become weary in doing good" (Galatians 6:9).

Thankfully, fulfilling our calling from God brings us a deep sense of purpose and fulfillment...most of the time. But let's face it. Most callings are just plain hard. Your burden and calling may be to the lost, the poor, the unborn, the homeless, the fatherless, families, children, young men struggling to find their identity, or the breakdown of society and government. It's no mistake that God gave you that particular burden. You are His instrument. That's how He is redeeming the world.

As I said, my burden and calling is men's discipleship, but to be candid, about every two weeks or so I feel like giving up. This has gone on for decades. I often say, "God, I just don't get it. It seems to me that I want men to become disciples more than You do!" Of course, that's when I know it's time to take a break.

During one of those biweekly meltdowns, I was lying in bed trying to sleep, but instead, I tossed and turned because I was thinking about all the things in my ministry that appeared to be going backward. I pulled a Gideon and prayed, "God, I just need a sign."

That's when I heard the words form in my mind: *You've been faithful. Stay the course.* That's a good word for you too. If you've been faithful, stay the course.

The vision God put in your heart might be fulfilled right away, might happen tomorrow, or might not be fulfilled for twenty more years. So what should you do if it seems to be taking forever? The only thing you *can* do. Be faithful.

That's the only area we can influence. Timing belongs to God. Outcomes belong to God. So our job is to be faithful, not to produce a particular outcome.

You can't pull this off. But Jesus can. This is the holy grail for those times when you feel like throwing in the towel.

> Let us fix our eyes on Jesus, the author and perfecter of our faith, who for the joy set before him endured the cross, scorning its shame, and sat down at the right hand of the throne of God. Consider him who endured such opposition from sinful men, so that you will not grow weary and lose heart. (Hebrews 12:2–3)

Scenario 4: "It's Really Happening!"

You already know your burden, and you're acting on it because you understand God wants to redeem some broken part of the world through you. This is a great place to be, because you have the thrill of seeing God work through you.

My friend Victor, an American citizen born in Honduras, has a burden for Central America. He recently went on a missions trip to his native land. His team traveled to several mountain villages, most of which did not have electricity. They had to pack in a generator to run their laptops and projector.

In one Honduran village thirty-four men assembled for a men's seminar. The pastor was astonished because no one could remember that many men coming together for a spiritual reason in the history of that village. In that region, a church typically has only two or three men and the rest are women.

In those remote villages, men don't respect women. Fathers routinely abuse their children, both physically and verbally. Against that backdrop, Victor spoke to those men about what it means to be a godly man, husband, and father.

And then something beautiful happened. The very next day, wives came to the pastor and said, "I cannot tell you what a change has taken place in just twenty-four hours."

Three months later a revisit to that village found the number of men attending its seven small churches had doubled, and 150 men were serving God and doing ministry. Many of those men have to walk three hours on dangerous mountain trails to get to the meeting place.

And it all started with a burden. God called Victor to step into a vacuum of knowledge about God and what it means to be a godly man, husband, and father in Honduras. He felt the burden of God and he went, and he has begun to redeem that part of creation.

Can you imagine how happy those wives and children are going to be over the next several decades because this one man was faithful not to refuse his burden? Victor understands that becoming the man God is making him to be compels him to respond to the burden God put in his heart. And it feels significant—like he really is God's redemptive agent in the world.

LET THE REJOICING BEGIN

When Nehemiah showed up in Jerusalem, the people were discouraged and weak. But Nehemiah soon managed to inspire them with his vision to rebuild the wall that had been broken down for so many years. He organized them and put them to work.

Some troublemakers, however, didn't much care for the idea of a secure Jerusalem. At first they tried to stop the work by ridiculing Nehemiah. When that didn't work, they threatened to attack. But Nehemiah would have none of it. Instead, he put half of his people to work with their swords at their sides while the other half stood guard. It was enough. His enemies backed down, and the work continued. And so, in the amazingly short period of fifty-two days, the wall that had been in ruins for a century was rebuilt and Jerusalem was made safe.

Whatever doubts Nehemiah and his comrades may have had when they were about to be attacked, it turned out to be one of the most rewarding seasons of their lives. Rebuilding the wall, and thereby restoring the city's dignity and safety, was a legacy they could look back on with pride and with gratitude to God. On the day they dedicated the new wall, "they offered great sacrifices, rejoicing because God had given them great joy. The women and children also rejoiced. The sound of rejoicing in Jerusalem could be heard far away" (Nehemiah 12:43).

I can tell you there's nothing like the thrill you get when you respond to the burden God has given you and see Him act through you. That's how I feel when I see men's lives change through the discipleship I'm helping to bring into their lives. I know this work is what I'm meant for, and it feels great to actually be doing it.

Becoming the man God wants you to be, however, is not principally about personal fulfillment. A man becomes himself by fitting into the larger perspective of what God is doing in the world. Our callings are about what God wants, what God is doing, what God is changing, what God is transforming.

As we answer the passionate calling God puts on our lives to change the world, we change too. We grow in dignity as men. We become more confident, more focused. We lose that nagging sense of purposelessness and, instead, experience the satisfaction of knowing that we're taking part in something that really matters, something that's close to God's heart—His big, audacious plans to redeem the whole world.

And when we answer the call, somewhere a wall gets built or rebuilt. Somewhere some broken part of the world gets redeemed. We do what the Master needs. And He gets the glory He deserves. So never refuse that burden, because that is how God is restoring the world.

For Reflection and Discussion

1. What is something that is breaking your heart, and why?

2. What was Nehemiah's burden, according to Nehemiah 1:3–4? And what did he do about it, according to the following verses:

   1:4 _____

   1:5 _____

   1:6 _____

   2:4–5 _____

   2:11, 17–18 _____

   4:7–9 _____

   4:16, 23 _____

   6:15 _____

3. With respect to the burden God has put on your heart, which of the following four scenarios best describes you? And what should you do based on what you've learned from Nehemiah? What is or could become your passionate calling? What have you learned or been reminded of from studying Nehemiah that can help you along, and why?

   Scenario 1: "I Don't Know What to Do"

   Scenario 2: "I'm Reluctant to Begin"

   Scenario 3: "I'm Trying, but to Be Honest, It's a Struggle"

   Scenario 4: "It's Really Happening!"

8

JOB

THE PRINCIPLE OF SUFFERING FOR NO APPARENT REASON

How God Molds Men Through Suffering

When one of my best college friends was in high school, he was driving too fast around a curve on a dirt road. He fishtailed, lost control of his car, and hit a tree. He has spent the rest of his life in a wheelchair.

A deep-in-debt man I know learned that his destructive spending sprees are linked to the manic-depressive disorder with which he must now learn to cope.

A middle-aged neighbor died suddenly of a heart attack, leaving a wife and three school-age children alone in the world.

A retired man lost most of his savings in the stock market crash and had to go back to work.

You have been through this kind of inexplicable suffering, are in it now, or will one day find your faith stretched to its limit. Suffering makes up such a large part of our lives.

Of course, we all treasure special moments, such as graduations, marriage, the birth of a child, and promotions. But what are we supposed to make of our sufferings?

Sometimes, of course, *we suffer for doing wrong.* We all get that. We yield to temptation from the world, our own sinful nature, or the devil, and so we suffer for our sins. We are not surprised that God disciplines His children as any loving father would do.

We also suffer for doing right. Christians are persecuted for their faith. For example, a young man I know was ridiculed for starting a Bible study at work. Another for taking a stand when his boss was blasting Christianity. But in cases like those, we can find strength from God's Word because we know we're doing the right thing.

- "If you suffer as a Christian, do not be ashamed, but praise God that you bear that name" (1 Peter 4:16).
- "Those who suffer according to God's will should commit themselves to their faithful Creator and continue to do good" (verse 19).

It's a third kind of suffering that's especially hard to come to grips with. It's when *we suffer for no apparent reason,* like some of the men mentioned above or because of natural disasters, accidental deaths, disease, handicaps, and so much more.

There just appears to be a lot of senseless evil and suffering in our broken world. Tragedies seem to strike at random and without respect to how much faith you have. And we're talking about deep and profound suffering and trials, not mere inconveniences.

These troubles make us wonder, *Does God know what I'm going through? Does He care? If He knows and cares, why doesn't He do something about it?*

What we find, if we look closely, is that suffering is an important part of how God molds us into the men He wants us to be. Which leads us to the principle this chapter is based on:

> God makes men by allowing us to gain through suffering what can be gained no other way.

Job is the man in the Bible and throughout history who's best known for asking questions about suffering. I find it hard to imagine that any of us have suffered more than Job, which is why we are going to talk about his life in this chapter.

But first, a word of caution: it would be outrageously insensitive to offer theological explanations to someone while he or she is going through profound suffering, such as when a soldier loses his legs, a spouse gets cancer, a worker loses his job, or a child dies. Broken hearts need love, not doctrine. So hopefully you are reading this before or after suffering. If you are going through profound suffering right now, feel free to come back to this chapter at another time.

A BIOGRAPHY OF SUFFERING

In Job 1 and 2, we learn that Job was a very wealthy man with extensive business interests in farming and livestock. He was also the father of seven sons and three daughters. If he lived in your community today, Job would be a respected husband, father, businessman, and Christian.

But then things began to go terribly wrong.

One day a messenger came to Job and told him that some raiders had stolen his livestock and killed all of his servants. While that messenger was still speaking, another messenger came and said that fire had destroyed another big part of his business empire and all of the employees. While the second messenger was still speaking, yet another messenger brought word that a raiding party had stolen a different herd of livestock and killed his servants. While the third messenger was still speaking, a fourth came and told him that a great wind had collapsed the building where his ten children had been holding a dinner party and they were all dead.

And then the final blow—Job's body broke out with sores from the top of his head to the tips of his toes.

Job went from *It couldn't get any better* to *It couldn't get any worse*. In despair, he sat down in an ash heap and used pieces of broken pottery to scrape at his sores.

Take a moment and think about something tragic you have been through.

In my case, one of my personal sufferings is migraine headaches. They are not as bad as they used to be, but I still take pills. When I was in business, I had migraine pills squirreled away everywhere. I had them in my glove compartment, my pockets, my briefcase, my desk, and at home. I kept pills everywhere because the pain could come suddenly and, if not caught right away, be excruciating. There have been many nights when I could not sleep because I was writhing in pain.

One day I sat down and read a book about migraines. I started weeping uncontrollably when the chapters described my symptoms and their effects. It was so overwhelming because I had never seen them written down in one place before. The author had written my biography of suffering.

I have been through seven or eight other major sufferings. You have been through your own sufferings too.

Perhaps God put the example of Job's suffering in His Word so none of us could ever say, "God doesn't understand what I'm going through." You may lose your business interests or investments. Some of us will see people we work with die unexpectedly. Some of us will have children tragically taken from us. For example, a man told me recently that his child died in a traffic accident. He was the driver. But Job suffered in a way that is almost incomprehensible.

Let's look at how he responded to such unspeakable pain. In his story we'll find insights into how God allows suffering to help mold us into the men we were created to be.

How Job Responded to Suffering

After his children were killed and all of his wealth destroyed, Job said,

> Naked I came from my mother's womb,
> And naked I shall return there.
> The LORD gave and the LORD has taken away.
> Blessed be the name of the LORD. (Job 1:21, NASB)

Job was clinging to his integrity. He was clinging to his faith. Verse 22 says, "In all this, Job did not sin by charging God with wrongdoing." Even after multiple severe tragedies struck, Job did not sin by blaming God.

But his woes were far from over. After his health failed, his wife said to him, "Are you still holding on to your integrity? Curse God and die!" (2:9). What must Job have been thinking at that moment? No doubt something like *I've lost everything, and now my wife has abandoned me too.*

But even when his wife turned against him, Job remained steady. He told her, "'You are talking like a foolish woman. Shall we accept good from God, and not trouble?' In all this, Job did not sin in what he said" (2:10).

And even that wasn't the end of his woes. Later his friends turned against him, assuming that Job must have brought on his own troubles by sinning. And still Job hung on to his faith, saying, "Though he slay me, yet will I trust in him" (13:15, KJV).

Not only that, but despite his misery, Job was confident that he would be vindicated:

[God] knows the way that I take;
>   when he has tested me, I will come forth as gold.
My feet have closely followed his steps;
>   I have kept to his way without turning aside.
I have not departed from the commands of his lips;
>   I have treasured the words of his mouth more than my
>   daily bread. (23:10–12)

Job's story is your story too. Even though you are a man of faith, even though you have walked with integrity, you are not immune from suffering for no apparent reason. If it hasn't already happened, someday something so painful will happen that you will wish you were dead.

At some point all of us suffer for no apparent reason. But that does not mean there is no reason. We see this truth in action when we look below the surface of what was going on in Job's life.

THE STORY BEHIND JOB'S SUFFERING

Even after Job was restored, he still never found out why he'd suffered so tremendously. But because we have the Bible, we do know why. The book of Job says Satan taunted God by claiming that Job would curse God if his blessings were taken away. And so God gave Satan permission to test Job with great suffering.

I said we know *why.* That's not quite true. Actually, we know *how* it came about. The actual reason why God allowed Satan to test Job so severely still remains hidden behind the veil of God's inscrutable will. "The secret things belong to the LORD our God," says Deuteronomy 29:29, "but the things revealed belong to us and to our children forever."

There is no formula for pain. And there is no formula to explain pain. There are only different types of suffering we can identify. For example, consider these men in Scripture, some of whom we've already met:

- Joseph was unjustly sold as a slave and imprisoned for a crime he didn't commit.
- David, a man after God's own heart, sinned deeply and was punished severely.

- Jeremiah was arrested and put in the stocks for speaking God's word (see Jeremiah 20:2).
- A man was born blind "so that the work of God might be displayed in his life" (John 9:3).

Let's be careful not to give formulaic answers for people's pain. I'm tempted all the time to attach reasons to people's sufferings. But except for when it's clear that we're suffering for doing right or wrong, we just don't know.

What we do know is this: Suffering is a part of God's plan of redemption. And it's also a part of His plan for making us into the men He wants us to be.

THE REDEMPTION OF SUFFERING

Job didn't know how his painful trials would turn out. On those sleepless nights when he was tormented by terror, he never knew which way his life would go. But we know because God graciously preserved his story for us.

After thirty-seven chapters' worth of reckless words between Job and his friends, the Lord spoke to Job: "Who is this that darkens my counsel with words without knowledge?" (Job 38:2). Then God peppered Job with questions such as "Where were you when I laid the earth's foundation?" and "Where does darkness reside?" (verses 4, 19) and about sixty more equally unanswerable questions.

Job was completely overwhelmed by the majesty of God. It was all he could do to humbly pray this prayer. Consider making it a prayer of your own.

I know that you can do all things;
>   no plan of yours can be thwarted.

You asked, "Who is this that obscures my counsel without
>   knowledge?"
>   Surely I spoke of things I did not understand,
>   things too wonderful for me to know.

You said, "Listen now, and I will speak;
>   I will question you,
>   and you shall answer me."
My ears had heard of you
>   but now my eyes have seen you.
Therefore I despise myself
>   and repent in dust and ashes. (42:2–6)

It's interesting. This man's integrity led to prosperity and made him a great man. But it was suffering that led him to hear God as he had never heard Him before. That applies to us too. We gain through suffering what we can gain no other way. Suffering allows us to hear the voice of God in a key that is audible only to the ears of the brokenhearted.

You know from your own sufferings, as Job did from his, that when you are at your lowest point and every other prop in your life has been removed or at least damaged, you have no one else to turn to but God. There's really nothing else you can do except throw yourself on the mercy and grace of the God who has unfailing love for you.

Though you don't understand exactly what God is doing, or why, you do understand that He is allowing it. And you know that He is good and that He will bring good from whatever causes you a dark night of the soul. As Romans 8:28 says, "We know that in all things God works for the good of those who love him, who have been called according to his purpose."

In Romans 8:28, God has taken an oath that nothing can happen to us that He will not redeem for His glory and our good. The Word of God promises that He will redeem your suffering. Whether in this life or the next, we do not know. Hebrews 11:13 gives us this sobering reminder about the generations who never actually saw the Promised Land:

> All these people were still living by faith when they died. They did not receive the things promised; they only saw them and welcomed them from a distance. And they admitted that they were aliens and strangers on earth.

In Job's case, however, God restored his circumstances during his lifetime. "The LORD blessed the latter part of Job's life more than the first" (Job 42:12). He acquired twice as much wealth, lived for another 140 years, and had seven more sons and three more beautiful daughters. Job went from *It couldn't get any worse* to *It couldn't get any better.*

If, like Job, you have been through great suffering, you know that what you've gained can never erase what was lost. But you also know that what you've gained is precious treasure and could have been gained in no other way.

Let's consider next what God wants you to know about suffering.

EVERYONE SUFFERS

From Genesis to Revelation, the Bible chronicles a great cosmic battle between the forces of good and evil that results in human suffering. The biggest challenge to the truth of Christianity has always been the problem of suffering and evil. The nonbeliever argues that because there is suffering and evil, there cannot be a loving God.

C. S. Lewis wrote that when he was an atheist, if someone had asked, "Why do you not believe in God?" he would've answered,

> Look at the universe we live in. By far the greatest part of it consists of empty space, completely dark and unimaginably cold.... It is improbable that any planet except the Earth sustains life. And Earth herself existed without life for millions of years and may exist for millions more when life has left her. And what is it like while it lasts? It is so arranged that all the forms of it can live only by preying upon one another.... [Man's] history is largely a record of crime, war, disease, and terror, with just sufficient happiness interposed to give them, while it lasts, an agonised apprehension of losing it, and, when it is lost, the poignant misery of remembering....
>
> There was one question which I never dreamed of raising.... If the universe is so bad, or even half so bad, how on earth did human beings ever come to attribute it to the activity of a wise and good Creator? Men are fools, perhaps; but hardly so foolish as that.[1]

Christianity doesn't claim to insulate us from suffering. If it did, then Christianity couldn't possibly be true. Instead, the Bible says everyone will suffer. Jesus said, "In this world you will have trouble. But take heart! I have overcome the world" (John 16:33).

The best Christian among us will have the same problems as the worst. Faith is not immunity from humanity. In fact, God allows Christians to go through the same trials as non-Christians so the world can see that Christ is real. Suffering is part of the deal.

But there's a larger truth I don't want us to miss: One of the chief ways we become the men God wants us to be is through the crucible of suffering.

Exactly what is to be gained by suffering?

TO GAIN WHAT CAN BE GAINED NO OTHER WAY

We may never find out exactly why we have to suffer, but there are dozens of gains that suffering can achieve. Here are some of the main reasons, and even benefits, for suffering that are listed in Scripture. Notice that it's more about what God gains through us than what we gain for ourselves, though both do occur.

- so that the work of God might be displayed in our lives, as in the case of the man born blind (see John 9:3)
- for God's glory, so that God's Son may be glorified through it, as in the raising of Lazarus from the dead (see John 11:4)
- so that our perseverance, our character, and the hope that does not disappoint may be developed (see Romans 5:3–5; see also Daniel 11:35)

- so that evil may be punished, as with the Israelites driving out the nations that occupied Canaan (see Deuteronomy 9:4–5)
- so that we may be delivered from bondage to decay and brought into the glorious freedom of the children of God (see Romans 8:20–21)
- so that we may comfort others with the comfort we ourselves have received (see 2 Corinthians 1:4; see also Luke 22:31–33)
- so that we will not rely upon ourselves but upon God (see 2 Corinthians 1:9)
- so that God may receive praise (see 1 Peter 1:6–7)
- because when we suffer, sin loses power (see 1 Peter 4:1–2)
- so that we may learn obedience (see Hebrews 5:8)
- because suffering will produce for us an eternal glory that vastly outweighs our light and momentary troubles (see 2 Corinthians 4:17)

It's well worth noting that there are no instances of meaningless suffering in the Bible. Even what appeared to be for no apparent reason actually had a reason. We saw this in the lives of Abraham, Joseph, Moses, Gideon, David, Solomon, and Nehemiah, and now we see it in the life of Job.

No man should ever seek out suffering—that would be foolish. Yet I hope by now you can embrace, not merely be resigned to, the inevitability of suffering. And because you know that great gains can come through suffering, you can find genuine comfort while you are in the throes of suffering.

He Knows, He Cares, and He Will Do Something About It

Although you are not insulated from suffering, you are under God's protection while you suffer. God loves you very much, and you can lean on Him as you walk through it. Here are some consoling truths about the questions raised at the beginning of this chapter about whether God knows what you're going through, whether He cares, and whether He can do anything about it.

Yes, God knows what you are going through. God is the one who said we must go through many hardships to enter His kingdom. God is the one who said, "Dear friends, do not be surprised at the painful trial you are suffering" (1 Peter 4:12). God is the one who said everyone who wants to live a godly life in Christ Jesus will be persecuted. God is the one who said you are blessed when people persecute you. Whatever it is you are going through, God most certainly knows what it is.

Yes, God absolutely cares about what you are going through. Jesus made it plain that in this world we will have trouble. But He also said we can come to Him when we are weary and burdened and find a level of relief that is incomparable to any earthly experience. He described it as "rest for your souls" (Matthew 11:29). Not only does God know what we're going through, but He cares deeply about it. In fact, the more we suffer, the more God will shower us with His comfort through Christ (see 2 Corinthians 1:5). So "cast all your anxiety on him because he cares for you" (1 Peter 5:7).

Yes, God has the power to do something about it. He is "sustaining all things by his powerful word" (Hebrews 1:3). He can and He will do something about whatever kind of suffering you are going through. I love what 1 Peter 5:10 says: "The God of all grace, who called you to his eternal glory in Christ, after you have suffered a little while, will himself restore you and make you strong, firm and steadfast." As we discussed in an earlier chapter, if He won't let a sparrow fall to the ground apart from His will, how much more will He watch over us?

Given all this, how should you respond?

YOUR RESPONSE

Here are some responses and attitudes toward suffering commended by Scripture:

- "Rejoice and be glad, because great is your reward in heaven, for in the same way they persecuted the prophets who were before you" (Matthew 5:12).
- "The apostles left the Sanhedrin, rejoicing because they had been counted worthy of suffering disgrace for the Name" (Acts 5:41).
- "You have been given…the privilege of suffering for [Christ]" (Philippians 1:29, NLT).
- We're invited to participate in "the fellowship of sharing in his sufferings" (Philippians 3:10).
- "Consider it pure joy, my brothers, whenever you face trials of many kinds, because you know that the testing of your faith develops perseverance" (James 1:2–3).

- "Who are you, O man, to talk back to God? 'Shall what is formed say to him who formed it, "Why did you make me like this?"'" (Romans 9:20).
- "If you have played the fool and exalted yourself, or if you have planned evil, clap your hand over your mouth!" (Proverbs 30:32).
- "Rejoice that you participate in the sufferings of Christ" (1 Peter 4:13).

Something as Small as a Hazelnut

Julian of Norwich was an orthodox Christian mystic who spent her life sequestered in a tiny room attached to a church in Norwich, England, during the late fourteenth and early fifteenth centuries. The church still exists to this day, although most locals don't even know about it, as my wife and I discovered when we crisscrossed Norwich trying to find it!

In her book, *Revelations of Divine Love,* Julian described seeing a small object in the palm of her hand about the size of a hazelnut. She asked, "What may this be?"

The answer came, "It is all that is made." Then she wondered how it continued to exist and not disintegrate.

Again the answer came, "It lasts and ever shall because God loves it."[2]

In that "little thing" she discerned three truths: God made the world, God loves it, and God sustains it.

I keep a bag of hazelnuts in my office for perspective. They remind me that God has not left us on our own. He knows what we're going through. He really does care. Whatever is happening, you're going to get through this. God will provide.

For Reflection and Discussion

1. What is something you've gained through suffering that you could have gained no other way? Are you suffering now, and if so, can you explain what you're going through?

2. Because we can read the story of Job in the Bible, we know how the terrible tragedies that struck him came about. But Job never did find out. And while we know the ending, he had no idea how the story would end. With that in mind, how do you respond to what he said and did in Job 1:21–22; 2:10; 13:15; 23:10–12; and 42:2–6?

3. What has been said in this chapter that helps you make better sense of suffering? How will you respond to future suffering differently because of the principle we've explored in this chapter?

PETER

THE PRINCIPLE OF
MAKING DISCIPLES

HOW GOD EQUIPS MEN
TO REACH OTHER MEN

We all know the problems—divorce, fatherless boys, domestic abuse, pornography, metal detectors in schools, rampage shootings, Wall Street corruption, racism, poverty, the normalization of sin on television. And of course that's just a small sample of the moral decay in our culture. Some of the stats are alarming:

- 48 percent of women are choosing cohabitation over marriage.
- 41 percent of babies are born to single mothers.
- 36 percent of children live in homes without their biological fathers.
- 18 percent of pregnancies are terminated by abortion.

- Church attendance has dropped to 17.7 percent overall and
  13.3 percent among men.[1]

Men, is there anyone who doubts that our culture is worse off
than it was twenty years ago? Common sense tells us that American
society is unraveling at an alarming rate.

God sees these problems too, and He has a solution. Making disciples is God's designated way to release the power of His gospel on every problem we face. But we have to do our part. The Scriptures frame
disciple making as a moral issue. By that I mean making disciples is a
choice between right and wrong, obedience and disobedience.

Does that statement sound harsh or arbitrary to you? Stay with
me. I think you'll see that how we face the truth about disciple making
will determine whether we become part of the solution for our world
or remain part of the problem.

As Christians, we get our moral authority from Scripture, so let's
refresh our memories with a few of the most familiar texts.

- "You will receive power when the Holy Spirit comes on you;
  and you will be my witnesses" (Acts 1:8).
- "Go and make disciples" (Matthew 28:19).
- "Teach these truths to other trustworthy people who will
  be able to pass them on to others" (2 Timothy 2:2, NLT).
- "As the Father has sent me, I am sending you [to make
  disciples]" (John 20:21).

No matter how violently it is attacked or apathetically it is dis-
missed, the truth of God just won't go away. The conclusion is in-
disputable. Discipleship is a moral issue. In fact, we could say this:
*Anything less than a plan to disciple every willing person is a catastrophic
moral failure.*

For some of us, disciple making is our main ministry. But as you can see, it is every Christian's mission and duty—starting at home. Failure to disciple at home leads to failure everywhere.

Why is discipleship so important? Problems get solved when the right kind of people are trying to fix them—disciples. So if we help people become who God created them to be, then they will be released to do what God created them to do. They will become servants of God and agents of change in our homes, workplaces, churches, and communities. They will populate our governments, school systems, health care, and businesses. Everything else is lipstick and rouge.

Men, we can do this. We can solve our problems by making disciples. God has a rewarding role for you to play. But before you can be a disciple maker, you need to know how. Jesus has a surprisingly simple plan to make disciples and then send us out to disciple others. Which brings us to the ninth principle of *How God Makes Men:*

> God makes men by a process of calling,
> equipping, and sending us so we can
> call, equip, and send others.

Disciple comes from the Greek word *mathetes,* which translates as "pupil" or "learner." When used in conjunction with Jesus, it came to mean an adherent to the person and teachings of Jesus—a follower.

Used as a verb, it's the process by which God *calls* us to salvation, *equips* us to live the Christian life, and *sends* us to live with Jesus and for His glory. An inherent part of the definition of a disciple is that we are *sent* to repeat the process and help others become disciples too.

I am sent. You are sent. That is fact.

What we do with that fact is choice.

MEN'S DISCIPLESHIP

Men's discipleship is especially important. The "men problem" has become a crisis that is virtually out of control. The collateral damage in families is staggering. Men under forty are especially vulnerable to an alien worldview that is gutting the institutions of marriage and family. Our government agencies, social sector organizations, and businesses are overstrained trying to cope with the downstream damage of an increasingly fatherless, angry, and dysfunctional generation.

There has to be a better way.

By all means, let's continue helping single moms, pregnant teenagers, and fatherless boys. We need more of that, not less. But we'll never solve these symptomatic problems without treating the underlying cause—that men don't understand biblical manhood.

I am so grateful that when my wife and I first visited our church, several mature Christian men were on the lookout for younger guys like me. Knowing what needed to be done, they took me under their wings and began to disciple me into biblical manhood and, from the start, gave me the vision to disciple others.

Hugh Lake preached the gospel simply. H. O. Giles and Bob Helmling modeled the gospel until I had to have it. God used Dan Stanley to bring me to conviction of sin. Jim Gillean invited us to be part of his small group, where my wife, Patsy, and I were equipped. I give glory to God for these men. And I trace it all back to my praying wife.

Jim in particular saw something in me that I didn't see in myself.

What really got me was that he believed in me more than I believed in myself. He spoke words of encouragement that I'd never heard before. That unchained something inside me. He gave me a vision to become the man God created me to be. That released the power to become a man I didn't even know was there. He started me down a path to become the man I wanted to be—a godly man, husband, father, and disciple maker.

God has given us a clear, simple prescription to bring men to maturity. It's for mature men to take younger men under their wings and show them how to walk the Christian life. Men are His method. He equips us to reach other men, because it takes a man to teach a man how to be a man.

Here's the good news. If we get men right, we will get marriages right. If we get marriages right, we will get families right. If we get families right, we will get the church right. And if we get the church right, God will change the world.

In a very real sense, the cure for everything starts with men's discipleship. That's the way Jesus saw it.

In this chapter, we're going to look at how the disciple-making process works. We know more about how Peter became a disciple and disciple maker than any other man in the Bible, so let's find out how it happened.

Calling Ordinary Men into an Extraordinary Relationship

Peter and his brother Andrew owned a small fishing business. Not long after Jesus began His public ministry, He said to them, "Come, follow me…and I will make you fishers of men" (Mark 1:17). Jesus simply invited them to start a relationship. As Peter heard those staggering words, his heart flooded with the prospect of finding a higher purpose for his life.

He took a sabbatical and left everything—like a short-term missions trip. He toured with Jesus. He witnessed firsthand the early miracles of Jesus. Peter saw Jesus cast out a demon, heal his mother-in-law of a high fever, and preach throughout Judea. When they returned home, Peter decided he needed to give some attention to his fishing business.

Not long after that, Jesus asked Peter for a small favor. Jesus was trying to speak to some people who had crowded around Him to hear the word of God. He saw two boats pulled up onshore by Peter and some other fishermen who were washing their nets. Jesus got into the boat that belonged to Peter and asked him to push a little offshore so He could teach the crowd.

When Jesus finished speaking, He told Peter to put out into deep water and let down his nets for a catch. That must have been an awkward moment: a carpenter telling a fisherman how to catch fish. Plus, every fisherman on the Sea of Galilee knew you catch fish at night, not during the day!

By this time, though, Peter had enough experience with Jesus to trust Him. So he said, "Master, we've worked hard all night and haven't caught anything. But because you say so, I will let down the nets" (Luke 5:5).

They took out the boat, let down the nets, and caught so many fish that their nets started to break. Then they signaled for the other boat to come help, and they filled both boats with so many fish that they started to sink!

When Peter saw what Jesus had done for him, he was unexpectedly overcome by emotion. Peter fell at His knees and said, "Go away from me, Lord; I am a sinful man!" (verse 8). He was, in a word, awestruck.

Once Peter called Jesus "Lord" and confessed his sinfulness, Jesus said, "Don't be afraid; from now on you will catch men" (verse 10). So Peter and the other fishermen pulled their boats up onshore, left everything, and followed Him. And so began the illustrious career of the man we associate with passion, boldness, courage, curiosity, and yes, impulsiveness and flaws.

How God Calls Men Today

I have a pretty good idea of what Peter went through, and I'll bet you do too. That's because not much has changed in the area of calling men to discipleship in two thousand years. The major difference between then and now is that instead of calling us in person, Jesus has raised up millions of witnesses—us—to help people understand His gospel and respond. Witnessing is simply taking people as far as they want to go toward Jesus.

Here's my calling story. Like Peter, I loved my work but wondered if there was any larger purpose to life. Was life just a random, senseless, pointless, wasted experience? At the time, it sure seemed like a futile and meaningless exercise. We're here, then gone. Life is hard, and then you die. So what?

But then God began to awaken within me a yearning to know—to really know—Him. I had often thought that if I ever had the chance, I would have dozens of difficult questions for God to answer. But that's not the way it happened. Not even close.

When I first started thinking seriously about God, I had pictured Him high but not *that* high, because at the same time I thought I was pretty high too. As I started to get to know the Lord, however, I realized He is so much higher and holier than I ever thought or imagined.

Then one day I felt I didn't even deserve to be in His presence. The glow of His glory was like a halogen floodlight that exposed what a sinful creature I am compared to His holiness. I felt shame and guilt to even be in the presence of something so heavy, so holy. Awestruck, I hit the deck. Like Peter, I said in essence, "Go away from me, Lord; I am a sinful man!"

But that awestruck moment of humility, faith, and repentance is precisely what Jesus is looking for—the starting point of how God makes men.

Of course, each of our stories is different in the details. There is no formulaic way of giving our lives to Jesus. But in one sense each of our stories is similar—the emptiness, the lack of meaning and purpose, the futility of it all, the anger, the lashing out, the loneliness, the existential pain, the drawing toward Jesus, the witnesses, hearing God's Word, the conviction of sin, the coming to an end of self, repentance, faith, surrender, and making Jesus Lord.

His challenge to us, like it was to Peter, is to follow Jesus—to give Him our lives and then be the witnesses who tell others how they can follow Him too.

Peter answered the Lord's call. But before Christ could send Peter out to make disciples, He first had to equip him for the task.

EQUIPPING ORDINARY MEN FOR EXTRAORDINARY
TASKS THROUGH AUTHENTIC RELATIONSHIPS

I've already mentioned that Jesus has a surprisingly simple plan to make disciples. We find it in Mark 3:14–15: "He appointed twelve—designating them apostles—that they might be with him and that he might send them out to preach and to have authority to drive out demons."

Jesus called Peter and the rest of the twelve disciples to be *with Him.* In other words, He called them into a relationship—a small group, a life-on-life community where they would become like brothers.

They would eventually spend three-plus years living, eating, working, playing, praying, and retreating together. They observed the life and teachings of Jesus. They saw His miracles. They watched how people responded and how lives changed. They were touched by His tenderness, kindness, and love. They marveled at His wisdom, restraint, mercy, and forgiveness. They were enraptured by the parables of the kingdom and by His description of His own death and resurrection. They practiced what they learned by going out in pairs, then reported back what had happened.

Jesus brought ordinary men together in authentic relationships where He equipped them to accomplish extraordinary tasks. That was, and is, the elegant simplicity of God's plan to make men who will be qualified to reach other men.

Jesus made it safe for His disciples to express their honest doubts and reservations and to ask questions. Peter was the curious one who often asked the questions that were no doubt on the minds of all the disciples:

- "Explain the parable to us" (Matthew 15:15).
- "Lord, how many times shall I forgive my brother?" (Matthew 18:21).
- "We have left everything to follow you! What then will there be for us?" (Matthew 19:27).
- "Tell us, when will these things happen?" (Mark 13:4).
- "Lord, are you telling this parable to us, or to everyone?" (Luke 12:41).
- "Lord, where are you going?" (John 13:36).
- "Lord, why can't I follow you?" (John 13:37).
- "What about him?" (John 21:21, referring to the fate of John).

Imagine how much we wouldn't know if Peter hadn't asked!

One day Jesus asked the disciples, "Who do you say I am?" In what is known as the Caesarea Philippi Confession (after the location where it was made), again it was Peter who responded, "You are the Christ, the Son of the living God." Jesus replied,

Blessed are you, Simon son of Jonah, for this was not revealed to you by man, but by my Father in heaven. And I tell you that you are Peter, and on this rock I will build my church, and the gates of Hades will not overcome it. (Matthew 16:15–18)

Peter's association with Him was having the desired effect. Peter was changing. He was being transformed by the renewing of his mind (see Romans 12:2). He was growing in spiritual maturity (see Ephesians 4:11–13). He was being equipped to live like Christ.

A Place for Flawed Men

Yet Peter also made many mistakes. A few moments later, Jesus began to predict His death. "I'm going to go up to Jerusalem," He said. "I'm going to suffer. I'm going to be killed. But I'm going to rise from the dead" (see Matthew 16:21).

Peter, who only moments before had declared his belief in the deity of Jesus with such humility and conviction, now took Jesus aside and scolded Him for saying such a thing. "'Never, Lord!' he said. 'This shall never happen to you!'" (verse 22).

Don't you love it? Haven't we all been there, telling God what's best for Him? If God didn't use flawed men, He wouldn't use any men at all.

Even though Peter was well on his way to becoming the man God wanted him to be, we can still see a lot of things that were not quite right in him. "Jesus turned and said to Peter, 'Get behind me, Satan! You are a stumbling block to me; you do not have in mind the things of God, but the things of men'" (verse 23).

Jesus didn't literally mean that Peter was Satan. He meant that Peter was saying the kind of thing that Satan prompts men to say from their sinful human nature. That's why Jesus said, "You do not have in mind the things of God, but the things of men."

There were, of course, other stumbles—like cutting off the right ear of the high priest's servant, denying three times that he even knew Jesus, and telling Jesus, "You shall never wash my feet!" (see John 18:10, 17, 25–27; 13:8).

Like Peter, you and I are going to stumble. To stumble is part of the process. That's inevitable.

Like a loving parent, God lets us experiment and fail. Jesus isn't put off by our spiritual immaturity. Quite the opposite. He expects it.

Think of it like this. If you have children, you knew long before you ever had them that they would be little sinners; but you still wanted them, right? And even when they sin, you still love them, don't you? You knew that they would sin and that you would have to discipline them, right? And the reason you discipline them is that you love them—you want the best for them, right? When they sin, your desire is always to forgive them and to restore them, isn't it? That's exactly what God is like. Even though He knew we would be sinners, He never stopped wanting to have us as His children. He is committed to helping us grow up into mature disciples by being with Him.

How God Equips Men Today:
Eight Months with Dan

As it was in the days of Jesus, God is still equipping men the same way He always has. Equipping is simply bringing people together around Jesus and watching Him change the way they think and what they do.

Today, we still gather in venues that let us develop authentic, growing relationships with God and each other—places like church services, adult learning classes, home groups, house churches, men's small groups, couples' Bible studies, one-on-one meetings, informal get-togethers over lunch or coffee, book groups, retreats (for example, men, marriage), trainings (leadership, evangelism), and special classes (parenting).

There's also the equipping that takes place in private through spiritual disciplines such as Bible reading, prayer, Scripture memory, and fasting.

Here's the takeaway: anything that will move a man along toward spiritual maturity is equipping. Take Dan, a new friend of mine. Dan was my driver at a conference where I was one of the speakers, and we really bonded. After knowing Christ for many years, he had his eyes opened at the conference to the urgent necessity of men's discipleship. In the next chapter, you'll be astonished to learn how Dan came to Christ, but you'll be just as amazed at how God has been equipping him in the last eight months once he decided to start discipling other men.

Even though he had virtually no experience, Dan was willing to step out in faith. He started a small group with five men from his church to capture the momentum from the conference where we met. Those men and their wives—especially their wives—liked the changes they experienced, so four months later Dan suggested they put on a men's retreat for their church of 130 people. No one was more surprised than Dan when thirty men showed up! To capture that momentum, they started another small group, and seven men signed up.

A woman in his church said her husband was interested in the small group but was too full of anger to take the step of joining. So Dan and his small group canceled one of their meetings and met with the man, who also brought two friends. The guys in Dan's small group shared how their group had started, how they had bonded, and how their wives were seeing big changes in them. All three men signed up on the spot.

In the months after the men's retreat, Dan worked to restart a church men's breakfast that had gone dormant six years ago. While on vacation, he shared what he was doing with a group of men. Now those men plan to start their own small group. Another man invited him to speak at his church about how the men in Dan's church have changed so much in such a short time. At work, Dan has been talking with and praying for a man asking questions about God. He said, "I asked him if he wanted to pray and ask God into his life. He wants to but asked for a little more time. I will be there for him. I am surprised at the amount of great things that are happening in our church. It's truly a blessing to us all."

And all of this in eight months. Why did this happen? Because Dan is so touched by what God is doing in his life and family and in the lives and families of those other men. His passion for making disciples is based entirely on his own experience—and it's contagious!

God's challenge to each of us, like Peter and Dan, is to let Him change the way we think and what we do, then equip others to do the same.

Finally, let's turn our attention from calling and equipping to sending.

THE EXTRAORDINARY MINISTRIES OF ORDINARY MEN

A main purpose for equipping us is to send us to reach others who will, in turn, reach still others. In other words, spiritual multiplication. Here's how Paul said it to Timothy: "Teach these truths to other trustworthy people who will be able to pass them on to others" (2 Timothy 2:2, NLT).

No one grasped this simple plan of Jesus better than Peter. Mark 3:14 tells us that Jesus picked twelve men not only to be with Him but also to send them to make disciples.

The words *Peter* and *bold* go together in many people's minds. He was a gigantic figure in the early church. Galatians 2:9 calls him a pillar of the church. While Abraham is the father of our faith, it was through Peter that God first made it known that the gospel of Jesus includes everyone, not just Jews. His extraordinary ministry is recorded in the book of Acts.

For example, after the Resurrection, Peter preached to a huge crowd of people. After his first sermon, *three thousand* people responded and became followers of Jesus (see Acts 2:41).

When Peter was traveling the country, he found a paralyzed man who had been bedridden for eight years. Peter said, "Aeneas...Jesus Christ heals you. Get up and take care of your mat" (Acts 9:34). Aeneas immediately got up, and as a result, *many people who lived in that area turned to the Lord.*

Once there was a woman named Tabitha. She was a disciple known for doing good and helping poor people, but she died. Her friends asked for Peter. When he arrived, he "sent them all out of the room; then got down on his knees and prayed. Turning toward the dead woman, he said, 'Tabitha, get up'" (Acts 9:40). She opened her eyes and got up. *The story went viral, and many people believed in the Lord.*

These are merely a handful of the astonishing things Peter did. Yet before Jesus invited him to be part of His small group, Peter, like Dan, was an unknown man leading a small life. So how do we account for his success in making disciples?

Remember the tours with Jesus, the trips when the disciples went out in pairs to learn the ropes, and how Jesus gave them an example to follow? Peter had such amazing results because he was trained by the Master.

Here's the rest of the story. Once Peter started achieving success teaching and preaching about Jesus, the religious establishment had Peter and John seized and jailed. But that was like throwing gasoline on a burning fire. The number of men who believed exploded to five thousand (see Acts 4:4). The next day Peter and John were questioned, but the Holy Spirit gave Peter powerful words to boldly proclaim the good news. Here's what happened next: "When they saw the courage of Peter and John and realized that they were unschooled, ordinary men, they were astonished and they took note that these men had been *with Jesus*" (Acts 4:13).

Now we know how Peter, an unschooled, ordinary man, had such an extraordinary personal ministry. He had been with Jesus. That was the center of God's training strategy from the start. And that's how you can have an extraordinary personal ministry too. Simply gather around the person of Christ, preferably in the company of a few like-minded men, and watch Him change the way you think and what you do.

DISCIPLESHIP STARTS AT HOME

By now, I'm sure you're not surprised that God sends men in much the same way He has been sending them down through the centuries. Once you've been enlisted in God's army and learned how to clean and shoot your weapon, you're going to be deployed. Sending is simply going wherever God wants you to go to do whatever God wants you to do.

Of course, making disciples is not the only thing God sends us to do. But in this chapter we're focusing on the Great Commission, or "making disciples," part of sending. Let's consider the priorities of making disciples.

First, making disciples starts at home. Your most important ministry is to your wife (if you have one). A friend of mine was having marriage problems. He came to one of our conferences and got inspired to disciple men. Since that brought him joy and home brought him distress, he started putting more and more time into discipling men and spending less and less time with his wife. When he asked me about it, I said, "I don't want you doing ministry to men until you get your ministry to your wife right." To his credit, he went back and put his own marriage in order. Today, he has a flourishing ministry to men.

Second, after your wife, your most important ministry is to your children (if you have any). A man's number-one discipleship group must be his family. No amount of success anywhere else can compensate for failure here. God has ordained you to disciple your children. If they don't get discipled, that one's on you. You are God's designated way to release the power of the gospel in your children.

Finally, once you have your own house in order, then you can have a disciple-making ministry to others. All kinds of people need discipleship. But let me make a special plea. You see, one of the greatest needs in our day is to disciple younger men. An incident from the animal kingdom illustrates this.

When elephants overcrowded South Africa's Kruger National Park, the government authorized killing adult elephants and relocating their offspring to other parks.

As the orphaned male elephants became teenagers, they were clueless about what normal elephant behavior looked like. When their testosterone levels spiked, the orphaned bulls turned aggressive. In one park they savagely killed thirty-nine rhinos. A park ranger watched as a young bull elephant intentionally knocked over a rhino and trampled it. The situation was out of control.

Then rangers brought several adult bull elephants into one of the parks. Just by being themselves, these animals mentored the younger bulls, demonstrating to them what normal male elephant behavior looked like. No more rhinos were killed after the mature bulls arrived.[2]

It's not easy to become a man. Many young men today have grown up as practical orphans. They've been left to guess at what normal male behavior looks like. The faith of young men is under severe attack. That's where the battle is raging. And frankly, mature Christian men are just not getting the discipleship job done. Consider these challenging words:

> If I profess, with the loudest voice and the clearest exposi-
> tion, every portion of the truth of God except precisely that
> little point which the world and the devil are at that moment
> attacking, I am not confessing Christ, however boldly I may
> be professing Christianity. Where the battle rages the loyalty
> of the soldier is proved; and to be steady on all the battle-field
> besides is mere flight and disgrace to him if he flinches at that
> one point.[3]

So consider discipling some younger men. That's a place where you are needed.

Of course, you can make disciples anywhere, anytime. In the course of a normal week, we each will come into personal contact with scores of people who have lost their way. A man so unsure of himself that he avoids eye contact, an angry salesclerk, a beggar standing beside an interstate off-ramp, a man who has committed adultery, a guy in your church addicted to [you name it], a ticket taker at the movies who never smiles, a neighbor who neglects his kids, an abusive boss.

My friend Jim and I had been going to a favorite restaurant for about a year. Over that time, we had been building a relationship with a waiter and nudging him toward the Lord. His name was Sean, and we'd found out quite a bit about him. When he was in high school, his father had had an affair and his parents divorced. He was now twenty-six, had a four-year-old daughter, and was divorced because his wife had cheated on him. In other words, he'd had two terrible betrayals.

One Friday, Jim made a reservation at the restaurant and requested Sean as our waiter. That day I said to Sean, "You know, I've been married for forty years to my wife and I love her more today than the day we got married." I did not plan to say it, but it just came out.

He said, "Do you really mean that?"

Jim chimed in, "Yeah, he does, and I feel the same way about my wife!" That was the turning point. Suddenly a year's worth of investing in an authentic relationship opened the door.

After a moment of reflection, Sean asked, "How can I find a wife like that?"

I asked, "Do you really want to know?"

He said, "Yes."

I said, "The way you find a wife like that is to find a woman who loves God."

Comprehension spread across his face, and he began to tell us about how he had grown up in the church. He retained a fragrant memory of things spiritual, but he had gotten away from this component of his life, and he knew he needed to get back to it.

I added, "However, there's a catch, because if you want to marry a woman who loves God, what do you think a young woman who loves God is looking for?" I paused for effect. "She is looking for a young man who loves God."

Again comprehension spread across his face. A great door had opened, and the Holy Spirit stepped through. Sean said he wanted to get information, he wanted to read books about spiritual things, he wanted to renew a journey toward God, and he wanted to change.

That's as far as I took it. My ministry that day was to give him a nudge. I trust God to bring other witnesses and disciple makers into his life. That's a good reminder: the fact that we can't do everything for someone is no excuse for not doing anything.

THE MINISTRY OF GIVING PEOPLE A NUDGE

Our job is to be faithful, not to produce a particular outcome. It's the ministry of giving people a nudge—whether that's calling them to live *in* Christ, equipping them to live *like* Christ, or sending them to live *for* Christ. Simply be with them—the people whom God has placed in your path. Nudge them along. Everybody deserves a nudge. And you're just the man who can do it!

For Reflection and Discussion

1. Can someone be a true disciple if he doesn't help others to become disciples too? Explain your answer.

2. What was the surprisingly simple method Jesus used to disciple Peter and the rest of the Twelve described in Mark 3:14? How effective was it, according to Acts 4:13?

3. Are you ready to step up to the challenge of making disciples? What are the key factors for you to be successful?

PAUL

THE PRINCIPLE OF A SURRENDERED LIFE

HOW GOD EMPOWERS MEN TO FULLY FOLLOW CHRIST

Two men met at an evening Bible study. One said to the other, "You look familiar. Haven't I seen you around my office building?"

With a playful twinkle in his eye, the second man said, "Yes. I am a disciple of Jesus disguised as a janitor."

In your city there are a lot of joyful men like this who quietly go about the business of leading passionate lives for the glory of Jesus Christ.

They're everywhere—waiting tables, fixing computers, pounding nails, picking up trash, selling cars, practicing law, delivering packages, managing stores, mowing lawns, and running small businesses. They're overflowing with purpose, meaning, joy, and yes, plenty of opposition and struggles. Yet these men are absolutely convinced their lives are going somewhere and making a difference. They're alive! You can't help but look at them with admiration, maybe even a touch of envy.

Perhaps you're one of these men. Or maybe you used to be one but now you've grown weary and lost your passion. Or maybe you've seen the joyful passion of men sold out to Christ and thought, *That's what I want!* But something is missing and you're not sure what it is.

Trevor, a young man in his late twenties, asked me to mentor him. On our fourth visit (long enough for him to size up whether or not he would trust me), he sat down and blurted out, "I have a mediocre business, a mediocre marriage, and a mediocre relationship with God." Trevor was already a Christian—that wasn't the problem. But he just couldn't see how he could ever become a joyful man passionately living for Christ. He was wrong.

In this final chapter I want to show you the amazing process by which God is helping Trevor become that joyful, all-in disciple of Jesus we all want to be—like the janitor I mentioned above. You'll learn (or be reminded of) how you can go wherever Jesus would go, whenever He wants you to go, to do whatever He would do. In fact, the creed of a servant is "Wherever, whenever, whatever." No reservations. No holding back. Increasingly surrendered.

The last principle we want to grab hold of is this:

> God makes men by forging us into
> humble servants who are increasingly
> surrendered to the lordship of Jesus.

Few men ever have been more passionate about following and serving Christ than the apostle Paul. He was an "on fire, let's get 'er done, do-your-duty, I can't keep it in / gotta let it out, press on, fight the good fight, finish the race" kind of guy. He was willing to go wherever and whenever God sent him to do whatever God told him to do.

We can learn a lot from Paul about the surrendered life. Let's start by looking at just how passionate he was.

THE PASSION OF PAUL

What comes to mind when you think of Paul? Is it his pioneering missionary work, his far-flung travels, his preaching to crowds who had never heard the name of Jesus, his religious pedigree and credentials, or perhaps the incredible body of work he wrote?

Maybe it's his tenacity in spite of prisons, floggings, beatings, stonings, great pressure to the point of despair, and being shipwrecked without losing faith. Maybe it's the opposition he faced from the very ones he was trying to help. Maybe it's his willingness to go without sleep, food, a warm blanket, or even enough clothes.

We know more about Paul than perhaps any other man in the Bible except Jesus. During a career that spanned thirty years, Paul spoke hot-blooded words that thunder off the pages of the Bible. Spend a few moments taking in the passion, zeal, and tenacity he revealed in these amazing words:

> We are hard pressed on every side, but not crushed; perplexed, but not in despair; persecuted, but not abandoned; struck down, but not destroyed. (2 Corinthians 4:8–9)

I have been crucified with Christ and I no longer live, but Christ lives in me. The life I live in the body, I live by faith in the Son of God, who loved me and gave himself for me. (Galatians 2:20)

For to me, to live is Christ and to die is gain. (Philippians 1:21)

Whatever was to my profit I now consider loss for the sake of Christ. (Philippians 3:7)

I want to know Christ and the power of his resurrection and the fellowship of sharing in his sufferings, becoming like him in his death. (Philippians 3:10)

I am not ashamed of the gospel, because it is the power of God for the salvation of everyone who believes: first for the Jew, then for the Gentile. (Romans 1:16)

I resolved to know nothing while I was with you except Jesus Christ and him crucified. (1 Corinthians 2:2)

I have become all things to all men so that by all possible means I might save some. I do all this for the sake of the gospel, that I may share in its blessings. (1 Corinthians 9:22–23)

Yet when I preach the gospel, I cannot boast, for I am compelled to preach. Woe to me if I do not preach the gospel! (1 Corinthians 9:16)

Paul had the same kind of slow-burning, inexhaustible faith that we saw in Abraham, Joseph, Moses, David, and Nehemiah. Let's look at where this irrepressible zeal came from.

THE GRATITUDE
THAT COMES FROM GRACE

When we first spot Paul in the New Testament, he was obsessed with stamping out Christianity. He traveled from city to city, breathing out murderous threats and arresting Christians. On one of those trips Paul had a dramatic encounter with Jesus. Here's how he retold his story some thirty years later to King Agrippa:

> In my obsession against them, I even went to foreign cities to persecute them.
>
> On one of these journeys I was going to Damascus with the authority and commission of the chief priests. About noon, O king, as I was on the road, I saw a light from heaven, brighter than the sun, blazing around me and my companions. We all fell to the ground, and I heard a voice saying to me in Aramaic, "Saul, Saul, why do you persecute me? It is hard for you to kick against the goads."
>
> Then I asked, "Who are you, Lord?"
>
> "I am Jesus, whom you are persecuting," the Lord replied. "Now get up and stand on your feet. I have appeared to you to appoint you as a servant and as a witness of what you have seen of me and what I will show you. I will rescue you from your own people and from the Gentiles. I am sending you to

them to open their eyes and turn them from darkness to light,
and from the power of Satan to God, so that they may receive
forgiveness of sins and a place among those who are sanctified
by faith in me." (Acts 26:11–18)

Paul clearly understood that the Messiah he had declared war
against had just confronted him. But to his utter surprise, instead of
getting what he deserved, he got something else—Jesus converted him
into a new man.

The foundation of Paul's passion? He couldn't get over the idea
that God would bend down so far to scoop up a man as unworthy
as himself. Here's how Paul, as a gray-haired man in his sixties with
three decades of Christian experience behind him, explained it to his
protégé, Timothy:

I thank Christ Jesus our Lord, who has given me strength,
that he considered me faithful, appointing me to his service.
Even though I was once a blasphemer and a persecutor and a
violent man, I was shown mercy because I acted in ignorance
and unbelief. The grace of our Lord was poured out on me
abundantly, along with the faith and love that are in Christ
Jesus.

Here is a trustworthy saying that deserves full accept-
ance: Christ Jesus came into the world to save sinners—
of whom I am the worst. But for that very reason I was
shown mercy so that in me, the worst of sinners, Christ
Jesus might display his unlimited patience as an example

for those who would believe on him and receive eternal life.
(1 Timothy 1:12–16)

Simply put, Paul never got over grace. Grace means getting the mercy we don't deserve and not getting the justice we do deserve. Fortunately, just like Paul, we don't get what we deserve either. We also are offered grace. Is there any man among us so dull that at the end of any given day he would actually want what he deserved?

Christianity only makes sense once you see yourself as a sinner who needs grace. *Lord, don't give us what we deserve; give us grace!*

The starting point for the life we all want is our personal conversion experience. Of course, the circumstances of every conversion are different in some respects, but they are always the same in the essentials of repentance and faith. Some men have dramatic conversions, but many men who grew up in Christian homes can never remember a time when they didn't trust Christ.

I was drawn to explore Christian faith because of the emptiness of success. To my utter disappointment, I learned that the emptiness of success feels eerily similar to the ache of failure. I was meeting all of my business goals, but like Solomon, I hated my life. I was gagging on success.

Since I grew up going to church, I assumed I understood Christianity. I knew who Jesus was and I believed in Him, but I had never given my life to Him. I knew very little about His identity, nature, character, and attributes. I certainly didn't think He had anything to say about my day-to-day life. And that was the problem. Our theology—how we understand God—affects everything, and bad theology will crush you.

Forged by Spiritual Growth

Typically when we first come to Christ, we feel a lot of excitement. But then most of us do what I did. As baby Christians, we try to have the best of both worlds. We try to have the best of what the Christian life has to offer without giving up our pursuit of the best of what the world has to offer. We tend to make a *partial* surrender of our lives.

I remember feeling like I was holding on to God with one hand while in the other was a big duffel bag filled with all my goals. I didn't want to let go of God, but I didn't want to let go of my goals either. The book of James describes that as being "double-minded" (James 1:8). We can pack lots of stuff into our duffel bags—ambition, reputation, control, health, money.

Nevertheless, we start to grow, because the same Spirit who converted us is now living in us to sanctify our lives and make us holy. Remember, equipping is simply bringing people together around Jesus and watching Him change the way they think and what they do.

But as we've learned, He's operating in Bible Time. Our transformation from a secular, moral, or even religious worldview to a Christian worldview is a lot like the work of raising a child. What parent doesn't know it takes a long time to raise a child to maturity?

You start reading the Bible, attending church, and participating in a small group. Then someone takes you under his wing to disciple you. Your understanding of God begins to change. Slowly at first, because you have a lot of baggage—a duffel bag full of it.

But as you learn more, your estimate of God becomes higher and higher. You realize that He is so much greater than you ever imagined.

You thought you would start to feel like you had a handle on God. Instead, you become overwhelmed by His attributes. You realize that He shrouds Himself in great mysteries.

Then one day, because of how big God has become, you realize that you are not as big as you once thought you were. And your estimate of yourself starts to shrink. You become lower and lower in your own eyes.

There is a widening gap between your understanding of who God is and who you are. And it just keeps growing wider and wider. Let's call this "the awe gap."

As the gap continues to grow, you become increasingly overwhelmed with reverence and awe toward God. Eventually you get to where you can't take the weight of His glory anymore. You are humbled. You don't feel worthy of His grace. This is what Paul felt when he quoted John the Baptist speaking about Jesus: "He is coming after me, whose sandals I am not worthy to untie" (Acts 13:25; see Mark 1:7). It's what the tax collector felt when he "would not even look up to heaven, but beat his breast and said, 'God, have mercy on me, a sinner'" (Luke 18:13). It's what Peter felt when he said, "Go away from me, Lord; I am a sinful man!" (Luke 5:8). All of your growth, you realize, comes through grace by the Holy Spirit. You fall on your face.

Eventually the awe gap grows so wide that you realize you're putting some real distance between you and the temptations of this world that once had a grip on you. The demanding teachings of Scripture that once put you off become intriguing. Jaw-dropping verses like the following make your pulse quicken:

The greatest among you will be your servant. (Matthew 23:11)

Whoever wants to be first must take last place and be the servant of everyone else. (Mark 9:35, NLT)

Anyone who wants to be my disciple must follow me, because my servants must be where I am. And the Father will honor anyone who serves me. (John 12:26, NLT)

If you do not carry your own cross and follow me, you cannot be my disciple. (Luke 14:27, NLT)

You cannot become my disciple without giving up everything you own. (Luke 14:33, NLT)

If any of you wants to be my follower, you must turn from your selfish ways, take up your cross, and follow me. (Matthew 16:24, NLT)

When you were a baby Christian, you probably read these verses. Unfortunately, if you are like most of us, what you did next was ignore them. They didn't make sense to you. They were just too far afield from your level of spiritual maturity. Sure, you believed they were true, but you just didn't have the spiritual maturity yet to embrace them. So you set them aside.

But as the awe gap continues to grow, the hard teachings actually start to make sense to you. You think, *I would love to live like that.* But you're not quite there yet.

SEEKING THE GOD WHO IS

Because we rarely release ownership of our lives on our own (even if we want to), God organizes a crisis to "assist" us in making a full surrender to the lordship of Jesus. Now, this is certainly not the pathway for every man, but in my experience it is for most of us. Suffering compels us to seek the God that success makes us think we don't need.

It could be a marriage crisis, a crisis with our children, a health crisis, a money crisis, or any one of dozens of other problems that drive that last bit of willfulness out of us.

For me, it was a business crisis. When I was a real estate developer, I took big gambles. As I described in an earlier chapter, when a major recession hit, I was overleveraged and my world started to crumble. One day while sitting in the rubble of my collapsing business, I was struck by an idea that I believe is the greatest lesson I've ever learned:

> There is a God we want, and there is a God who is. They are not the same God. The turning point of our lives is when we stop seeking the God we want and start seeking the God who is.

I had received Christ, but it dawned on me: *Morley, what were you thinking? Did you really think any amount of reinventing God in your imagination to be the God you wanted Him to be would have one iota of impact on His unchanging nature and character?*

It finally sank in. I had wanted to change God, but God wanted to change me. He wanted me to follow Jesus with my whole heart: wherever, whenever, whatever. That's what He wants for all of us—a full, total, complete surrender to the lordship of Jesus. Let me explain what I mean.

THE GREAT SURRENDER

Adrian Rogers, a famous twentieth-century Baptist pastor, once went on a missions trip to Romania. Over the course of two weeks, he bonded with his interpreter but hadn't learned much about his thoughts. So toward the end of the trip he asked, "Tell me, what do you think of American Christians?"

"I don't want to talk about it," came the strange reply. This, of course, only made Dr. Rogers more curious, so he began to press him for an answer.

Finally the interpreter capitulated. "Well, okay then, but you're not going to like my answer. I don't think you Americans understand what Christianity is all about. Back in the 1960s you started to use the word 'commitment' to describe your relationship with Christ. However, any time a word comes into usage, another word goes into disuse."

He continued, "Until the 1960s, you Americans talked about 'surrender' to Christ. Surrender means giving up control, turning over all to the Master, Jesus. By changing to the word 'commitment,' your relationship with Christ has become something you do; therefore you are able to keep control. Surrender means giving up all rights to oneself. You Americans don't like to do that, so instead you make a commitment."[1]

There are two ways to go. The first is to get bogged down by insisting you know what's best, trying to control the situation, exerting your will, trying to get your own way, and coming out on top. Filled with small ambitions, petty grievances, and easily hurt feelings, this is the way of the committed man.

The other way is to deny yourself, come humbly to the foot of the cross, give Jesus your life daily, fully consider the gravity of your times, and fit into the larger perspective of what God is doing in the world. Filled with humble gratitude, this is the way of the surrendered man.

By now, you might be wondering, *What does surrender look like in practice?* Consider the story of Dan, the friend I mentioned in the previous chapter.

Dan was one of those young men who had to guess at what normal is, especially in how to relate to women. He caught his fourth fiancée in the act with another man. He forcibly threw her out of his apartment. Unfortunately, he also kicked her, which ruptured her spleen. And so, at the age of thirty, Dan was sent to prison for a year.

A few months into his sentence, he had a private session with the chaplain, who asked, "Dan, do you know who Jesus is?"

He said, "Of course!"

The chaplain asked, "Do you believe in Him?"

He replied, "Yes."

Then the chaplain asked, "Have you ever given your life to Jesus Christ?"

He said, "No, I have never done that."

The chaplain suggested that Dan ponder if he was ready to give his life to Jesus. A week later, desperate for God, he repented, put his faith in Jesus, and surrendered his life to Christ. It's so like God to redeem such a horrible situation. Today, Dan is happily married to a strong, surrendered Christian wife.

Have you truly surrendered, not just committed, your life to Jesus

Christ? Maybe you have prayed a sinner's prayer; maybe not. Maybe you surrendered in the past, but you have taken back control of your life. In any case, be sure to settle this issue before you set down this book.

The great irony of surrender is that it leads not to defeat but victory.

You can surrender, or re-surrender, your life by humbly telling God in your own words that you desire to yield control of your life to Him in repentance and faith. Or, if you wish, you can pray this prayer:

> *Lord Jesus, I need You in my life right now more than I ever have. I have very little joy, peace, and passion in my life. I confess that I have been trying to have the best of both worlds, that I have been double minded, and that I have been seeking the God I have wanted and not the God who is. I am so sorry, and I repent. Please forgive me. Thank You for loving me so much that You would die for all my sins so that I can have eternal life. By faith I receive (or renew) my salvation and I surrender my life to You. Take control of my life. Make me into the kind of man I've been reading about in this book. I pray this in Your name, Jesus, and for Your glory. Amen.*

If you've just surrendered or re-surrendered your life, congratulations. The surrendered life is the foundation under everything we've been discussing in this book. Be sure to tell someone what you've done. If someone gave you this book, let him or her know. Tell your spouse, your pastor, your small group—anyone who will listen. The feedback you receive will strengthen your faith.

Let me add one suggestion. Because I am a rebel, as most men are, I realize that I must each day come humbly to the foot of the cross in a spirit of repentance and faith, once again making a full, total, and complete surrender of my life to the lordship of Jesus. Let me encourage you also to practice daily surrender.

Finally, once we raise our heads from making that full surrender, we are ready to take on our greatest role.

BECOMING A SERVANT

Paul is arguably the world's leading expert on the surrendered life. What was his response to Jesus? It was to become a faithful servant. He said, "I became a servant of this gospel by the gift of God's grace given me through the working of his power" (Ephesians 3:7). He wrote, "It is required that those who have been given a trust must prove faithful" (1 Corinthians 4:2). At the end of his testimony before King Agrippa, Paul declared, "I was not disobedient to the vision from heaven.... I preached that they should repent and turn to God and prove their repentance by their deeds" (Acts 26:19–20).

To fully surrender our lives to Jesus is to become a servant. Yes, we are sons of God, but we are also His servants. A servant is no longer preoccupied with the question "What do I want?" Instead he's asking "What does the Master need?" This is no small difference.

A servant doesn't serve God to get a reward (although there are many). A servant is simply doing his duty. Jesus said, "So you also, when you have done everything you were told to do, should say, 'We are unworthy servants; we have only done our duty'" (Luke 17:10).

The chief test of whether or not you are a servant is whether you're willing to be treated like one. If we never make a sacrifice for Jesus, then how will either one of us know that we really love Him?

So whatever is asked of you—whether time, money, a menial task, or something that is inconvenient or "beneath" you—the questions to ask are, *What does the Master need? What would a servant do?*

Practically speaking, what would it look like to live this way—to follow Jesus and serve Him wherever and whenever for whatever?

STAY WHERE YOU ARE

In most cases, the Lord wants us to stay in the place where we were when He first called us to salvation, doing the same things we were do-ing before (see 1 Corinthians 7:17) but with a whole new perspective toward our family, work, church, and community.

Take our work, for example.

At Steffi Graf's induction into the International Tennis Hall of Fame, her husband, Andre Agassi, told a story:

> We were on the road, and I looked out our hotel window
> from the upper floor of a very tall high-rise. I could see the
> rooftop of an old and beautiful cathedral. It was stunning
> with its carved stone and marble all done so perfectly. I could
> not believe the work of art I was seeing, and I wondered, *How
> many years did it take them to create this, and what drove them
> to be this committed?*
>
> Then I began to appreciate something greater. I realized
> when this rooftop was built, it was by far the tallest building.

And in an age long before airplanes or skyscrapers, these artists believed each day as they went about their work that no human being, no one set of eyes would ever see their creation. How could they not have cut one corner?[2]

We know the answer. They were absolutely sure that their work *was* being seen. By an audience of One. When we do our work with excellence, without cutting corners, men will sometimes see our good works and give glory to God. But He will always see.

To God, our work *is* serving the Lord. So, "whatever you do, work at it with all your heart, as working for the Lord, not for men.... It is the Lord Christ you are serving" (Colossians 3:23–24).

You see, there is no such thing as a "secular" job. He equips and sends us to be carpenters, plumbers, custodians, doctors, computer repairmen, truck drivers, lawyers, politicians, soldiers, and so on. Every vocation is holy to the Lord. Our work is not merely a means to other ends. There is intrinsic value in the work we do.

I've told the men at our Bible study, "If you are out of work or underemployed, you should be networking to find work here among the brothers, because work is righteous. You should never be embarrassed about letting men know that you need work."

Or take our families as another example. Hannah Whitall Smith wrote in *The Christian's Secret of a Happy Life* about a woman who got all excited about doing great works for God. But this woman had to go be a parent to two sick and irritable children.[3] If you have a similar responsibility as a parent, then that is the great calling you have from God. In fact, that may be the greatest thing you will ever do in your life.

Here's an example of building a personal ministry in the community. After meeting with some men in a small group for a couple of years, I suggested we each think about how we could serve Jesus in politics, education, or civic affairs. I volunteered for civic affairs and joined the Winter Park Chamber of Commerce. I prayed, *Lord, now what?*

Then someone said, "Would you like to be on the program committee?"

And I said, "Okay."

After a while I prayed, *Lord, could You please rehearse with me what I'm doing here?*

Six months passed and one day the committee chair resigned. Someone asked me, "Would you like to chair the program committee?"

I said, "Okay."

After a while I prayed, *God, why do You have me here?*

Not long after, I sensed a leading to start a prayer breakfast at Thanksgiving to share Christ with community leaders. Everyone liked the idea, so we went ahead. The first year about 150 people attended. Several received Christ. In the twenty-five years I chaired the Leadership Prayer Breakfast, hundreds of business leaders became Christians. And with new leadership, the annual tradition continues to be an important date on our community calendar.

God sustained my passion to serve Jesus for a quarter century! But it all started with a baby step—joining the chamber of commerce. Dan's great progress in the short span of eight months, as we saw in the previous chapter, also started with a baby step. That's about the only way it ever happens.

WRITING YOUR OWN EPIC STORY

In the beginning I made you a huge promise. I promised that if you would let ten men from the Bible mentor you, you could get past the shallow, cultural Christianity of our times and get to—or back to—a more biblical Christianity. I said that if you would take to heart the ten proven principles we find in these epic stories, then you would be well on the way to writing your own epic story.

So let's review what we've learned about how God makes men, and then take stock.

From Abraham we learned about *faith*—that God makes men by showing us how we can believe Him anyway in the face of what seem like impossible circumstances. Joseph taught us about *perseverance*— that God makes men by orchestrating even the toughest circumstances of our lives for a greater good.

Then we turned to Moses to teach us about *transformation*—how God makes men by taking us through a humbling process that fundamentally changes the way we think. After that, we looked at the story of Gideon to learn about real *strength*—and saw that God makes men by turning our weakness into strength in such a striking way that only He can get the glory.

The sobering story of David reminded us about *discipline*—how God makes men by doing whatever it takes to correct and restore us when we go astray. Then we turned to Solomon to learn about true *happiness*—that God makes men by making it impossible for us to find lasting happiness in any pursuit apart from Him.

In the story of Nehemiah we learned about how God *calls* men to action—that God makes men by turning what breaks our hearts into a passionate calling to help redeem some broken part of His world. In the story of Job we gained insight into *suffering*—that God makes men by allowing us to gain through suffering what we can gain no other way.

When we came to Peter, we learned the compelling principle of *discipleship*—how God makes men by a process of calling, equipping, and sending us so we can call, equip, and send others. Finally, through the passionate story of Paul, we learned about *surrender*—that God makes men by forging us into humble servants who are increasingly surrendered to the lordship of Jesus.

And that's how God makes men!

So how did you do? Were you able to absorb and embrace these ten proven principles? As we've seen time and time again, it's a process, isn't it? Now, as you set down this book, choose to let God continue to make you into the man He created you to be. Invite Him to mold your inner being in ways that release His power in every direction and detail of your life.

As you turn back to your life, I pray people everywhere will see you as a man who has been marked by the

faith of Abraham,
perseverance of Joseph,
humility of Moses,
courage of Gideon,
heart of David,
wisdom of Solomon,
zeal of Nehemiah,
integrity of Job,

boldness of Peter, and

passion of Paul,

for the glory of Christ and no other reason. Amen.

Reflection and Discussion Questions

1. Are you (a) a joyful man living a surrendered life for the glory of God, (b) a man who was once like that but who has lost his passion, or (c) a man who has yet to really find God's way of becoming God's man? Explain your answer.

2. Did you pray, or have you previously prayed, to fully surrender your life to seek the God who is? Explain your answer. If you have never done so, what's still standing in your way? (If nothing, go back to the section "The Great Surrender" and pray the prayer of surrender.)

3. Practically speaking, what would you like to do differently to demonstrate that you are willing to be treated like a servant? What does the Master need from you?

DISCUSSION LEADER'S GUIDE

It's easy to start a group to discuss *How God Makes Men* and lead a lively discussion by following these guidelines:

1. *Plan on meeting for ten weeks—one week for each chapter in the book.* Your group may be an existing Bible study, fellowship group, prayer group, or adult education class (women can be included). Or you may want to start a new group.

2. *How to start a new group.* Photocopy the table of contents and the questions at the ends of a couple of chapters, and give copies of these to the men you want to meet with. Ask them if they would like to be in a discussion group that would read the book and answer the discussion questions at the end of each chapter. This can be a group from work, church, your neighborhood, or a combination. The optimum group size is from eight to twelve men (assuming some men will have to miss a week occasionally). If the group gels, you may want to suggest that the group continue to meet after you are finished studying *How God Makes Men.*

3. *Distribute a copy of the book to each member.* Identify the first chapter as the reading assignment for your first meeting, and ask the group members to be prepared to answer the questions at the end of the chapter. Close with a prayer. Always adjourn on time.

4. *At your first meeting, strongly challenge your men to read the chapters ahead of time by telling them this story:* A men's

small-group leader once said, "The men who read the book chapter we study before they come to our small group are growing, and those who don't read it are stagnant. The stagnant ones just can't understand why their lives are not changing."

5. *Suggested meeting format.* Begin with an icebreaker question, such as "Anyone have a particularly good or tough week?" For a one-hour meeting, a good schedule to follow would be the following:

Discuss icebreaker question (five minutes).

Discuss the questions at the end of the chapter
(forty-five minutes).

Pray as a group (ten minutes).

6. *Have coffee and soft drinks available.* If you meet over breakfast or lunch, allow an extra twenty minutes for eating, if possible.

7. *Leading a discussion.* The key to a successful discussion group is your ability to ensure that each member gets airtime. Your role is to encourage each man to share his thoughts and ideas on the weekly chapter. If a group member asks an off-the-subject question, simply suggest that you discuss that issue at a separate time. If someone rambles too much, privately ask him to help you draw out the more shy members of the group. Take each question in order, and make sure everyone has the opportunity to comment. If you have a shy member, take the initiative and address him by name—for example, "John, how would you answer question 3?"

8. You don't have to be an experienced Bible teacher to lead a discussion about *How God Makes Men.* If someone asks you a

question beyond your scope, simply say so and move on. Your role is to facilitate a discussion, not teach the group.

9. Check out additional resources, such as the article "How to Lead a Weekly Men's Small Group" at PatrickMorley.com.

Send me an e-mail at patrickmorley@maninthemirror.org if you have any questions!

ACKNOWLEDGMENTS

Writing and publishing a book is a labor of love and ten thousand details. I would like to thank my team.

First and foremost, I thank my beautiful wife, Patsy, who acted as my sounding board, offering both encouragement and wisdom.

My only literary agent for my entire career has been Robert Wolgemuth and his agency, Wolgemuth & Associates, Inc. Thank you, Robert, Erik, and Andrew Wolgemuth, Austin Wilson, and Susan Kreider, for always knowing the next right step.

I'm deeply indebted to the entire WaterBrook Multnomah team. My special thanks to Ken Petersen and David Kopp for embracing me as a men's author and catching the vision for this book to help men discover, or rediscover, how God makes men. I would also like to thank Carie Freimuth and Lori Addicott and the stellar teams you oversee for bringing such energy and creativity to this project. I can't believe how invested you get in your authors. I thank God for you. Steve Reed, thank you for your longtime friendship and partnership with Man in the Mirror's Books! by the Box ministry to churches. Allison O'Hara, you have been my champion since day one. You're a rainmaker. Thank you, Ashley Boyer, for your diligence on my behalf to get the word out. Kris Orr, you nailed the cover design on the first round. Awesome! Chris Sigfrids, I'm so grateful for your help to integrate media and technology into this project. And thank you, Laura Wright, for managing all the production details and for making such a confusing process seem like a walk in the park. Eric Stanford, you did a stellar job line editing the manuscript. Kevin McMillan, I love what you've done with PatrickMorley.com. Because of you, I know that every leader, pastor, and man who needs to know about this book will. Thank you. I love you all.

Thanks to my colleagues at Man in the Mirror for making it possible for me to pursue my love for writing: Al Lenio, Bill Chapman, Brett Clemmer, Brian Russell, Carol Hetrick, Christina Angelakos, Aime Cochran, Corrie Cochran, Dave Hamilton, David Delk, Jeff Kisiah, Jamie Turco, Kimberly Massari, Laraine Irvin, Lucy Blair, Roddey Roberts, Ruth Cameron, Scott Russell, Sharon Carey, Tom Hingle, Tracie Searles, Jim Seibert, and all of our area directors.

And also to our board of directors: Dr. Pete Alwinson, Bill Helms, Sidney Hinton, Fred Mateer, Larry Mattingly, Jimmy Pendley, and Todd Woodard Sr. Thank you so much for making it possible for me to write.

Notes

Chapter 1

1. This is also when God changed his name from Abram to Abraham.

Chapter 2

1. Charles Colson with Ellen Santilli Vaughn, *Kingdoms in Conflict: An Insider's Challenging View of Politics, Power, and the Pulpit* (Grand Rapids, MI: Zondervan, 1987), 68.
2. Brent A. Barlow, "Marriage Crossroads: Why Divorce Is Often Not the Best Option: Rationale, Resources, and References," *Marriage & Families,* January 2003, http://marriageandfamilies. byu.edu/issues/2003/January/divorce.aspx.
3. Edwin H. Friedman, *Generation to Generation: Family Process in Church and Synagogue* (New York: Guilford, 2011), 69.

Chapter 5

1. G. I. Williamson, *The Westminster Confession of Faith for Study Classes* (Phillipsburg, NJ: Presbyterian and Reformed Publishing, 2004), 126.

Chapter 6

1. The same Hebrew word means both "revere" and "fear."

Chapter 8

1. C. S. Lewis, *The Problem of Pain* (New York: HarperOne, 2001), 1–3.

2. Julian of Norwich, *Revelations of Divine Love, Motherhood of God,* trans. and ed. Frances Beer (Suffolk, England: D. S. Brewer, 1999), 29–30.

Chapter 9

1. Women choosing cohabitation over marriage: Casey E. Copen, Kimberly Daniels, and William D. Mosher, "First Premarital Cohabitation in the United States: 2006–2010 National Survey of Family Growth," *National Health Statistics Reports,* no. 64, April 4, 2013, www.cdc.gov/nchs/data/nhsr/nhsr064 .pdf. Babies born to single mothers: "Unmarried Childbearing," Centers for Disease Control and Prevention, January 2013, www.cdc.gov/nchs/fastats/unmarry.htm. Children living in homes without their biological fathers: Rose M. Kreider, *Living Arrangements of Children: 2004,* Household Economics Studies, US Census Bureau, February 2008, www.census .gov/prod/2008pubs/p70-114.pdf. Pregnancies terminated by abortion: Karen Pazol et al., "Abortion Surveillance—United States, 2009," *Morbidity and Mortality Weekly Report,* Centers for Disease Control and Prevention, November 23, 2012, www.cdc.gov/mmwr/preview/mmwrhtml/ss6108a1.htm?s _cid=ss6108a1_w. Church attendance drop: When asked, "Did you attend church within the last week?" many polls show around 40 percent of people indicated they had. However, when a different question to adjust for social desirability

bias was asked, "What did you do last weekend?" only 17.7 percent of people indicated that they had attended church. The proportion of women to men in church is 45 to 34. So this research would indicate that actually 13.3 percent of men attend church every week, or roughly 16 million men fifteen years of age and older. Cathy Lynn Grossman, "At Nation's Churches, Guys Are Few in the Pews," *USA Today,* July 25, 2008, http://usatoday30.usatoday.com/news/religion/2008 -07-23-males-church_N.htm; and C. Kirk Hadaway and Penny Long Marler, "How Many Americans Attend Worship Each Week? An Alternative Approach to Measurement," *Journal for the Scientific Study of Religion* 44, no. 3 (August 25, 2005): 307–22, http://onlinelibrary.wiley.com/doi/10.1111/j.1468 -5906.2005.00288.x/abstract, cited in Rebecca Barnes and Lindy Lowry, "7 Startling Facts: An Up Close Look at Church Attendance in America," ChurchLeaders.com, www.church leaders.com/pastors/pastor-articles/139575-7-startling-facts-an -up-close-look-at-church-attendance-in-america.html?p=1.

2. "The Delinquents," CBS News, February 11, 2009, http://m .cbsnews.com/fullstory.rbml?catid=226894&feed_id=0& videofeed=36.

3. Elizabeth Rundle Charles, *Chronicles of the Schönberg-Cotta Family* (New York: M. W. Dodd, 1865), 321.

Chapter 10

1. Adrian Rogers, personal correspondence, 1998.

2. "Andre Agassi's Speech at Steffi's Hall of Fame Induction," YouTube video, 8:12, International Tennis Hall of Fame

Induction Ceremony 2004 filmed by *In Tenn Video Tennis Magazine,* posted by "mmsshh777," April 5, 2007, www .youtube.com/watch?v=ob_eU-J99HU.

3. Hannah Whitall Smith, *The Christian's Secret of a Happy Life* (Chicago: Moody, 2009), 38–39.

ABOUT THE AUTHOR

For decades Patrick Morley has been regarded as one of America's most respected authorities on the unique challenges and opportunities facing men. Through his speaking and writing, he is a tireless advocate for men, encouraging and inspiring them to change their lives in Christ.

In 1973, Patrick founded Morley Properties, which for several years was one of Florida's one hundred largest privately held companies. During this time, he was the president or managing partner of fifty-nine companies and partnerships.

In 1989, he wrote *The Man in the Mirror,* a landmark book rooted in his own search for purpose and a deeper relationship with God. With over three million copies in print, *The Man in the Mirror* captured the imaginations of men worldwide and was selected as one of the hundred most influential Christian books of the twentieth century. Altogether, Patrick has written twenty books and more than 750 articles. He has appeared on several hundred radio and television programs.

In 1991, Patrick founded Man in the Mirror, a ministry that has helped thirty-five thousand churches impact the lives of twelve million men worldwide. Their vision is "for every church to disciple every man" through local area directors who help churches disciple men more effectively. He speaks to men daily through the radio program *The Man in the Mirror Radio Minute,* which is carried on seven hundred stations nationwide.

In addition, Patrick teaches a Bible study every Friday morning to approximately ten thousand men—150 men live in Orlando,

Florida, and the others are reached through a webcast to all fifty states and throughout the world.

"The ministry of Man in the Mirror exists," says Patrick Morley, "in answer to the prayers of all those wives, mothers, and grand-mothers who have for decades been praying for the men in their lives."

Patrick Morley graduated with honors from the University of Central Florida. He has earned a PhD in management, completed postgraduate studies at the Harvard Business School and Oxford University, and graduated from Reformed Theological Seminary. He lives in Winter Park, Florida, with his wife, Patsy. They have two married children and four grandchildren.

His weekly video Bible study, articles, daily devotionals, radio program, books, and e-books can be found at PatrickMorley.com. You can follow him on Facebook at facebook.com/PatrickMorleyAuthor and on Twitter @patrickmorley. His ministry websites are ManInThe Mirror.org and AreaDirectors.org.

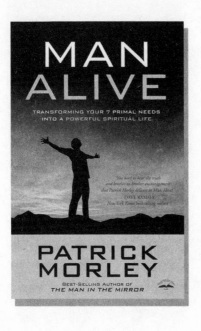

Man Alive is a practical, biblical, and highly motivating guide to personal transformation. Patrick Morley identifies your seven most deeply felt needs as a man and then guides you to experience spiritual growth in each area. This straight-talking book is for any man who wants to move beyond spiritual mediocrity.

Read an excerpt from this book and more at www.WaterBrookMultnomah.com.

In this 8-week DVD Study Resource based on the core book, Patrick Morley uses an informal setting interwoven with video clips to discuss the key insights of *Man Alive* and lead viewers in an interactive learning experience. Suitable for personal or group use.

In this "quick-start" overview of *Man Alive*, Patrick Morley shares the poignant story of his struggle to reconcile with his father and emphasizes how embracing God's unconditional love brought him the freedom and healing he was looking for. Available in packs of 10, ideal for churches, small group distribution, and men's outreach ministries.

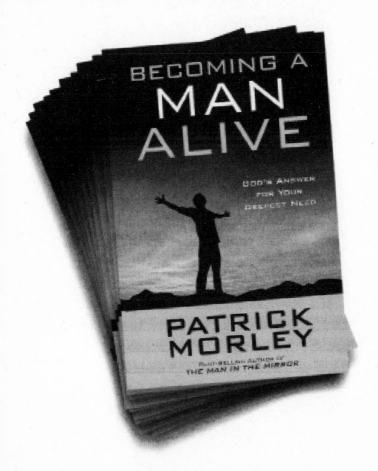

Additional resources available at
ManAliveBook.com